Refined by Fire

Refined by Fire

Rethinking Essential Teachings in Scripture

Robert P. Vande Kappelle

WIPF & STOCK · Eugene, Oregon

REFINED BY FIRE
Rethinking Essential Teachings in Scripture

Copyright © 2018 Robert P. Vande Kappelle. All rights reserved. Except for brief quotations in critical publications or reviews, no part of this book may be reproduced in any manner without prior written permission from the publisher. Write: Permissions, Wipf and Stock Publishers, 199 W. 8th Ave., Suite 3, Eugene, OR 97401.

Wipf & Stock
An Imprint of Wipf and Stock Publishers
199 W. 8th Ave., Suite 3
Eugene, OR 97401

www.wipfandstock.com

PAPERBACK ISBN: 978-1-5326-6236-2
HARDCOVER ISBN: 978-1-5326-6237-9
EBOOK ISBN: 978-1-5326-6238-6

Unless otherwise noted, Bible quotations are from the *New Revised Standard Version of the Bible*, copyright © 1989 by the Division of Christian Education of the National Council of the Churches of Christ in the United States of America. Used by permission.

Manufactured in the U.S.A.   08/14/18

Contents

Preface | vii

Session 1   Introduction | 1
Session 2   Rethinking Truth | 9
Session 3   Rethinking Faith | 17
Session 4   Rethinking God (the Sacred) | 29
Session 5   Rethinking Jesus | 43
Session 6   Rethinking Scripture | 63
Session 7   Rethinking Creation | 82
Session 8   Rethinking Evil, Sin, Death, and Hell | 108
Session 9   Rethinking Salvation, Heaven, and Eternal Life | 129
Session 10   Rethinking the Church, Its Nature, Mission, and Composition | 150

Appendix: James Fowler's Stages of Faith | 165
Bibliography | 167
Subject/Name Index | 171

Preface

I am a teacher by profession. For forty years I have taught at the college and graduate levels. However, teaching is not just something I do; teaching is my identity. My passion for learning led me to consider a career in religious studies, a choice that was confirmed by my fondness for the subject matter and because my initial teaching experiences created moments that were lively and true. I learned early on that the best teachers—the most effective—are committed to the *process* of education, a task that revolves around two priorities: (1) commitment to the pupil—as person and as learner—and (2) commitment to the joy of learning, to ever-fresh insights and possibilities. An effective teacher in the field of religious studies provides students with tools for inquiry and keeps the conversation going, not arriving at conclusions too quickly or using authority to clinch an argument. I try to follow that advice in this workbook, and I trust you too will value that approach as you read further.

While this workbook contains new material, it represents an anthology of sorts, for it contains an amalgam of theological comments and questions found in some of my previously published writings, notably *Beyond Belief* (2012), its discussion guide, *Iron Sharpens Iron* (2013), and *Securing Life* (2016), my text on the Bible. Readers who desire to pursue topics presented in this workbook are encouraged to consult those books and my commentaries on individual books of the Bible.

PREFACE

Notes for Participants

This discussion guide is grounded in the conviction that humans have the capacity to transcend conventional spirituality to a genuine and wholesome faith that is dynamic rather than static, future-oriented rather than past-oriented, and affirmed rather than passively acquired. This capacity is fueled by three principles:

1. That life is more important than death – this principle encourages us to pursue life-enhancing opportunities.

2. That whatever does not grow dies – this principle encourages us to remain open to change and newness.

3. that all truth is God's truth – this principle encourages us to remain open to truth wherever it may be found and wherever it leads.

Refined by Fire is written for those who affirm the value of lifelong spiritual growth, realize the limits of logic, and embrace the paradoxes in life. Such people see life as a mystery and often return to sacred stories and symbols, though without being confined to a theological box. This phase, identified by James Fowler as "conjunctive faith," is often discovered or reached in midlife, though sooner by some.[1] If you are prepared to grow spiritually, morally, and intellectually, I encourage you to embark upon the journey promoted in this guide.

Consider journaling during these next twelve weeks. To do so effectively, you will want to make time for silence and meditation. A good place to start is with your hopes and dreams. Be honest with your thoughts and feelings without ignoring your fears and repressed secrets (Swiss psychiatrist Carl Jung called this your "shadow"). Embrace all aspects of your being. Set aside the mask (Jung called it the "persona") behind which you hide from others and even from yourself. Transparency will facilitate the process of becoming healthy and whole.

Each chapter (session) follows a threefold pattern:

- *Getting Started* (an initial assignment for class participants)
- *Gaining Momentum* (a narrative section for gaining perspective)
- *Going Deeper* (questions for discussion or further reflection; leaders may select questions from this list they deem most helpful for group discussion)

1. See the appendix.

Preface

Participants should examine the assignment in advance of class, preferably one week beforehand. Participants and leaders alike should answer the questions that comprise the initial assignment, writing in advance their answer in their journal and being prepared to share their views with others during class time. [*Note*: leaders need to decide in advance if they want to include the results of these assignments in class, and if so, when.]

Notes for Leaders

Fire is difficult to control. However, if the fire comes from God (see Mal. 3:2–4; 1 Cor. 3:12–13; Rev. 3:18–19), or if the fire is God (see Heb. 12:29), then the refinement is intentional and the result holy and pure. This guide encourages humility, openness, respect, vulnerability, and a high degree of interaction among participants. The discussion questions are engaging and appeal to various levels of intellectual and spiritual awareness.

People who choose to attend a Bible study do so for a wide variety of motives and bring with them varied levels of readiness and ability. When individuals are invited to attend this group, they should be made aware from the beginning that this is not an indoctrination, meaning that answers are not necessarily assumed or always readily available, and that this is not a study where the leader does all the work of preparation and presentation. Every participant is expected to have read the appropriate material in *Refined by Fire* prior to each session.

Given the busy schedules most people have, there may be times when participants come to a session with minimum preparation. You should not compromise the expectation of adequate preparation, because the experience for the whole group will suffer if the reading is not taken seriously. In such situations, encourage persons who have not read the material or done the homework assignments not to participate in the discussion until others have had a chance. Also, when working in small groups, try to ensure that those who are not prepared are distributed among the groups rather than grouped together.

Some participants will have had a lot of experience with the Bible and theology, while for others this may be their first experience with such study. It is important for each person to feel that he or she belongs to the group. Encourage both experienced and inexperienced participants to be mindful and appreciative of each other. One way to ensure full participation is to ask participants to keep a journal, to write in it regularly, and to bring it to each

Preface

session. The journal will be used to record the weekly homework assignment as well as notes on their reading and on class interaction.

It is important that leaders prepare their own session plan appropriate for their group. This study is designed to be completed in ten sessions (with the Introduction as the opening session), each *60 to 75 minutes in length*. Each session follows a fourfold pattern:

1. *Opening*, 5 minutes (a time of prayer and scripture reading, run by the leader or by someone appointed in advance; the leader may ask if there are any prayer requests).

2. *Overview*, 15 to 30 minutes (this can be in the form of a presentation by the leader or in a group discussion on the topic of the homework assignment).

3. *General or small-group discussion*, 20 to 30 minutes (depending on the size of the class, the leader may divide the class into groups of threes or fours to discuss one or more questions from the "Going Deeper" segment).

4. *Closing*, 5 to 15 minutes (run by the leader or by someone appointed in advance). This may include a report and general discussion on the small-group activity, a time of reflection (see "Takeaway" statement below), or a comment by the leader and a closing prayer). During the optional time of reflection, ask participants to identify and record in their journal their takeaway (key insight) from that week's reading or from their group discussion (give the class 3 minutes of silence to formulate their takeaway and 5 minutes to share).

5. *Fellowship*. Depending on the setting, the session may close with a time of fellowship and refreshments. If the leader/host so chooses, a time of fellowship may precede the session.

If sessions last *45 to 60 minutes*, the recommended time allotments and activities should be adjusted accordingly.

Depending on the interests of the participants, study groups may modify the ten-session pattern by eliminating some of the sessions, by rearranging the topics, or by expanding into two or more sessions longer chapters such as Session 7, which contains a discussion on the relationship between religion and science.

Session 1

Introduction

Getting Started

Homework Assignment: Answer the following question, writing your answers in your journal. Be prepared to share your views with others in the class. 1. Examine Fowler's stages of faith, found in the appendix. Assess his model. Where do you find yourself on his scale? Where would you like to be? (*Note*: At the conclusion of this study you will be asked to revisit this topic and to rate your progress from start to finish).

Gaining Momentum

From time immemorial, in every age, a set of questions has persisted, perplexing human beings. What is going on in the universe? Is there any point to it all? Why are we here? Is there any purpose to our lives? How should we live? Does God exist? Where did the universe come from? Why does anything exist at all? Why is there so much suffering? Why do we die? Do we live on after death? How can we find release from suffering and sadness? For what can we hope? These have been called life's "big questions"; philosophers speak of them as "ultimate questions." They are the ones that never go away.

It is the main business of religion to answer the big questions. This is why, even when we try to distance ourselves from it, we remain intrigued by religion. Religion responds to the preoccupations that arise when one's life comes up against barriers beyond which ordinary—including scientific—ways of coping cannot take us. For our purposes, therefore, religions may be understood very simply as pathways or "route-findings" through the ultimate limits on our lives. These limits include not only death and meaninglessness but also anything that threatens our wellbeing, anything that stands between us and lasting peace or happiness.

To accomplish this task, every generation of believers benefits by re-examining its theology, thereby providing society with vision. A theology that is stagnant reflects a religion that is limited in both usefulness and effectiveness. The sociological, ecclesiastical, and theological concerns of the Reformation and the Enlightenment are largely behind us, as are the battles between modernists and fundamentalists, and there are more critical issues now at stake. Fundamentalist claims (inerrancy, young earth, literalism, dispensationalism, premillenial rapture eschatology) have set themselves up for attack by critical scholars, producing individuals bent on discarding the baby with the bath water when they encounter evidence that their strict upbringing may not be up to the task of explaining in the post-reformation, postmodern world. We can do better than that.

In this book, I wish to celebrate the many voices of scripture, written over a span of a thousand years from a variety of sociological and theological perspectives, and also the potential wisdom that can result when a group of twenty-first-century readers, also with varying sociological and theological perspectives, commit to join one another in honest, loving, and respectful discussion regarding theological topics such as the nature of God, Christ, scripture, truth, faith, evil, sin and salvation, heaven and hell, creation and evolution, the role of the church, and the future of the human race.

Life on planet earth is fragile, and our lives are immensely complex. Many issues divide us and many problems exhaust our resources. Can we as individuals make a difference? Can a small group, centered on biblical study and committed to honest and intelligent dialogue, move our society one step closer to a better and more hopeful future? As Van Jones, the television pundit, stated in an interview with TIME magazine: "Can we have a better set of debates, a more meaningful set of debates, *and actually get somewhere*?"[1]

---

1. Jones, "8 Questions," 56.

Introduction

A Defining Moment

Several years ago nine students, all seniors, joined me around a large old table in a seminar room for a course titled "The Development of Western Christianity." The topic was "The Sources of Authority for Modern Christians." The assigned reading featured the well-known epistemological approach called the Wesleyan Quadrilateral, which enumerates four sources of theology within the Christian tradition—scripture, tradition, reason, and religious experience—and the students were asked to prioritize them and to support their choice.

One fellow, preparing for the Christian ministry, began the discussion by arguing that scripture should be given top priority. The books of the Bible, he stated, are the basis of all Christian belief and practice, since all were inspired directly by God and therefore provide the highest degree of authority. All sources of authority should defer to biblical revelation.

The next student questioned that conclusion. Admitting that scripture is central to Christianity, she noted that the biblical canon was produced by the church and therefore should be included under the category of tradition. In her estimation, tradition, understood as comprising scripture, should have priority for Christian belief and practice.

Another person brought up an equally valid point: tradition, including scripture, comes bound in cultural and historical context and requires interpretation in order to be applied meaningfully to contemporary life. Since interpretation must be filtered through a variety of lenses, including human reason, one could argue that reason stands as the final and foremost source of authority for modern Christians. Several students found this to be persuasive, while recognizing that not all aspects of faith derive from human reason or can be subjected to the authority of reason.

The last person to speak, while agreeing that reason should be held in high esteem, particularly where theological beliefs might be shown to contradict logic or scientific conclusions, noted that logic and reason are not exclusively objective phenomena. Rational people, after all, disagree, and in a global and pluralistic world they increasingly concede that there are—and always have been—many different "rationalities." Thus, while affirming the centrality of reason, she concluded that reason could not claim the final word. In all cases, experience has the first and final word.

We left class pondering that final insight. Does reason, together with scripture and tradition, derive ultimately from experience? Our exercise seemed to support that conclusion, for none of the students had prioritized or substantiated their organization of the four categories in the same way. Subjective experience, it seems, lies at the heart of human consciousness and fashions reality as we know it. What we experience, we are. What we are, we think. What we think, we create. What we create, we become. What we become, we express. And what we express, we experience.

This exercise reminds us that to live and think fully, human beings need to find harmony within, firing on all cylinders of their selfhood. In his 1976 book, *Forgotten Truth*, the renowned scholar of comparative religions, Huston Smith, delved into the "primordial tradition," the common, fundamental experience of humankind, as found in the core teachings of the world's religions, identifying therein four levels of selfhood: body, mind, soul, and spirit. We will explore these levels in Session 7, understanding how they correlate with the four levels of reality. At his point, I simply emphasize the importance of connecting body and spirit for living fully, and of connecting head and heart (soul) for thinking wisely.

Whatever Does Not Grow Dies

There is in every human an impetus which, when nourished, seeks health and wholeness. Healthy human beings are said to go through discernible stages of growth throughout their lifetime. According to psychologist Erik Erikson, psychosocial development proceeds by critical steps. Each stage is marked by crisis, connoting not a catastrophe but a turning point, a crucial period of increased vulnerability and heightened potential. At such points, achievements are won or failures occur, leaving the future to some degree better or worse but in any case, restructured. As humans grow by progressing physically, psychologically, emotionally, and even intellectually, so they undergo various stages of growth in their faith.

Out of one's individuality flows a spirituality that also yearns for growth and expression. What Erikson contributed to our understanding of the stages of psychosocial development, Jean Piaget to the stages of cognitive development, and Lawrence Kohlberg to the stages of moral development, so James Fowler did for spirituality. He identified seven stages of faith, from stage zero, called "primal faith," when infants and toddlers develop (or fail to develop) a sense of safety about the universe and the divine, to a sixth stage called "universalizing faith." This level, rarely reached, characterizes those who live their lives to the full in service of others without any real fears or worries. Most people plateau at what Fowler calls the "synthetic-conventional" stage, one arising in adolescence. At this stage, authority is usually placed in individuals or groups that represent one's beliefs.[2]

The Translation Principle

Andrew Walls, perhaps the leading Christian missiologist today, has compared the nature of Christian expansion to that of Islam, the world's other great missionary religion. While both have spread across the globe claiming the allegiance of diverse peoples, Islam has demonstrated more continuity in its expansion and on the whole more success in retaining allegiance. With relatively few exceptions, the areas and peoples that accepted Islam have remained Islamic ever since, whereas the ancient Christian heartland, including Egypt and Syria, is now Islamic, and the European cities once stirred by the preaching of John Knox or John Wesley are now secular, filled with empty pews and abandoned churches. While it is possible to provide social and political explanations for this loss of allegiance, Walls points to an inherent fragility in Christianity itself, a built-in vulnerability that he labels "the translation principle in Christian history."

Unlike Islam, in which the effectual hearing of the Word of Allah (recorded as the Qur'an) occurs essentially through the medium of the Arabic language and through a scripture that cannot be translated, Christianity rests on the opposite premise, on a divine act of translation known as the incarnation: "the Word became flesh and dwelt among us" (John 1:14). In Islamic faith, God speaks to humanity in direct speech, delivered at a chosen time through God's chosen Apostle; such speech is immutable and unalterably fixed in heaven for all time. In prophetic faiths such as Judaism and Islam, God speaks; in the Christian faith, God becomes human. According to Walls, much misunderstanding has occurred due to the assumption that the Bible and the Qur'an have analogous status in the respective faiths. In fact, they are not analogous. It would be truer to say that the Qur'an is for Muslims what Christ is for Christians. "Christ, for Christians . . . is the Eternal Word of God; but Christ is Word Translated."[3]

---

2. Fowler's "stages of faith," including M. Scott Peck's simplified version, appears in the appendix.

3. Walls, *Missionary Movement in Christian History*, 27.

Incarnation is translation. When God in Christ became man, divinity was translated into humanity, as though humanity were a receptor language. Translation, however, is not a precise art but a high risk business. Exact transmission of meaning from one linguistic medium to another is continually hampered by structural and cultural differences. The words of the receptor language are pre-loaded, and meanings in the source language commingle with those of the receptor to create uncharted possibilities.

In the art of translation, another point arises: language is specific to a people or an area. No one speaks "generalized language," for all language is particular. Similarly, when divinity was translated into humanity, divinity did not become generalized humanity. Divinity was embodied in a particular person, in a particular locality, in a particular ethnic group, and at a particular place and time. The translation of God into humanity, whereby the sense and meaning of God was transferred, was effected under very culture-specific conditions.

This built-in vulnerability is engraved into the Christian foundational documents themselves. Whereas Islamic absolutes are fixed in a particular language, and in the conditions of a particular period of human history, the Christian revelation, including the words of Jesus himself, were transmitted not in Hebrew or Aramaic, the languages of first-century Palestinian Jews, but in translated form (Greek) in the earliest documents we have. This fragility is also linked with the essentially vernacular nature of Christian faith. For Christians, the divine Word is translatable, not once and for all, as though the translation could be captured in one time or in one place, but infinitely translatable. As Walls notes, "Christian faith must go on being translated, must continuously enter into vernacular culture and interact with it, or it withers and fades."[4] Bible translation as a process is thus both a reflection of the central act on which the Christian faith depends and of the commission that Jesus gave his disciples: "Go and make disciples of all nations" (Matt. 28:19).

As Christian faith is about translation, it is also about conversion. There is a real parallel between these processes. Translation involves the attempt to express the meaning of the source within the resources and working system of the receptor language. Something new is brought into the pre-existing language and its conventions. In translation, the original language and its system is effectively expanded, put to new use; but the translated element from the source language has also been expanded in

---

4. Walls, *Cross-Cultural Process in Christian History*, 29.

translation. The receptor language has a dynamic of its own and takes the new material to realms never touched in the source language.

Similarly, conversion takes existing structures and turns them to new directions. Conversion is not the substitution of something new for something old or the addition of something new to something old. Rather it is the re-orientation of every aspect of humanity—culture-specific humanity—to God. By nature, then, conversion is not a single act in time, but a process. It has a beginning, but we cannot presume to posit its end. Translation, whether of the Bible to other languages, or of Christianity to other cultures and mindsets, is also a process, with a beginning but no end. Christian diversity is the necessary product of the Incarnation.

Unlike Islam, whose Arabic absolutes provide cultural norms that apply across the Islamic world, Christian faith is repeatedly coming into creative interaction with new cultures, traditions, and different systems of thought. That means that Christianity's profoundest expressions are often local, vernacular, and temporal. Perhaps this is what Søren Kierkegaard, the existentialist Christian philosopher, had in mind, when he affirmed that it was "impossible to be a Christian in Christendom."

Going Deeper: Reflection for Participants

1. In your understanding, is there a significant difference between "spirituality" and "religion"?

2. Session 1 identifies some of life's "ultimate questions." What are your "big questions"? Is the role of religion to provide satisfactory answers to life's ultimate questions or simply to help us cope with life's uncertainties by offering hope and moral guidance? Explain your answer.

3. Throughout church history, thinkers have attempted to provide Christians with systematic theologies, attempting to frame biblical teaching in ways that make sense to human rationality. In your estimation, is it possible to harmonize biblical teaching in this way, or should we focus rather on appreciating the many voices of scripture, with their diverse sociological and theological perspectives? Support your answer.

4. Do you agree that every generation benefits by reexamining its theology? If so, where does one begin or conclude such a reexamination?

Should such a project be comprehensive and open-ended or be limited only to specific areas such as religious values and ethical standards?

5. If you consider yourself theologically conservative, what do you understand to be the theological agenda for your generation? If you consider yourself theologically moderate or liberal, what do you understand to be the theological agenda for your generation?

6. How would you answer the question, "What is the meaning of life"?

7. How would you prioritize the four sources of theology known as the Wesleyan Quadrilateral? Support your answer.

8. What does this chapter say about the "translation principle" in Christianity? What does this chapter say about the differences between Christianity and Islam regarding Christ and truth? Explain your answer.

9. Does this initial session raise questions you might want to address in future sessions? Is a topic missing that you would like to discuss in the future? If so, what is it?

10. In your estimation, what is the primary insight gained from this session?

Session 2

Rethinking Truth
Objective or Subjective?

Getting Started

Homework Assignment: Answer the following questions, writing your answers in your journal. Be prepared to share your views with others in the class. 1. Is truth objective (absolute) or subjective (relative)? 2. Is truth a divine construct, a human construct, or somehow both? Support your answer.

Gaining Momentum

For a society to work, rules and laws are necessary, with consequences for their violation. When we were children, most of us followed a code of conduct, explicit or implicit, such as obey your parents, get along with your siblings, and treat your elders with respect. Our parents gave us these rules, understood to be absolute, assuming that they passed the test of time because they worked, and that they worked because they were rooted in reality. The implication of such an assumption was that reality was essentially singular and uniform. According to this way of thinking, truth cannot be arbitrary or relative, because there is no continuum between right and wrong. Some things are naturally right, and others naturally wrong, with very few degrees of overlap or confusion.

This is how many of us think, because that is how our parents indoctrinated us from our youth, and rightly so. For their own safety and wellbeing, children need absolutes. They need to obey their parents and those in authority, and the best way to elicit obedience in children is to teach them to embrace values based upon the principle that right and wrong are polarities, distinct and without overlap; separated by a vast wall of separation, they are not to be breached or questioned. For that reason, most children grow up having a sense of right and wrong, of what is fair and unfair. This does not mean they always follow their conscience or conform their behavior to that code, but they seem to acknowledge the difference between right and wrong, knowing when they have crossed the line.

As we grow up, many of us begin to question the "life commandments" we received as children, and that can be good, necessary, and valid for becoming healthy adults. As Paul reminds us in his poetic masterpiece on love: "When I was a child, I spoke like a child, I thought like a child, I reasoned like a child; when I became an adult, I put an end to childish ways. For now we see in a mirror, dimly [lit. in a riddle], but then we will see face to face. *Now* I know only in part; *then* I will know fully . . ." (1 Cor. 13:11–12).

While interpreters tend to view Paul's face-to-face clarity as his longing for an eternal meeting with God in a future afterlife, I would like to suggest a different interpretation. When I hear these words, I envision a scenario in the present rather than in the distant future, empowered by God but occasioned by the hopeful results of collaborative encounters between adults who are spiritually, morally, and intellectually mature and open to newness and change. If, as Christian theologian Dietrich Bonhoeffer suggested, contemporary humanity has "come of age," can this mean that we humans already possess the capacity and the resources necessary to attain the future of which Paul spoke? I submit that such potential is present here and now, to those who approach truth dialectically, that is, who view truth as composed of elements varied and diverse, seemingly incongruous with one another. As the philosopher Hegel (1770–1831) famously noted, progress (social, moral, and even spiritual) occurs dialectically rather than linearly, through a process of struggle and interaction between polarities dubbed "thesis" and "antithesis." The resultant "synthesis" requires listening, appreciating, and learning from perspectives at variance from one's own. According to this scenario, Christians need no longer live out of the resources of Paul's first-century "now," but rather out of the potential of his twenty-first-century "then." If we humans can be said to have "come of age," spiritually, intellectually, and scientifically, isn't it time for those who follow Christ to unpack the implications of that shift?

While most authorities would agree that science and religion are still evolving, these disciplines have developed significantly since the first century. As contemporary physics reveals, nature is neither predictable nor uniform, and as contemporary philosophy reveals, truth is neither objective nor absolute. History is not guided by divine or human forces, as people of the West once believed, but by a process more random and circular than purposeful or progressive. We humans are caught in this vast evolutionary web of trial and error, our survival dependent upon adaptation and harmony rather than upon coercion and control. As even a casual conversation with people of different faiths, cultures, races, or social class reveals, relativity rules.

As a professor of religious studies teaching world religions and global spirituality, I uncovered numerous parallels between Christianity and other religions, including beliefs, practices, and historical development. This discovery convinced me that questioning beliefs, dogmas, and practices of other traditions while blindly accepting one's own is inconsistent, biased, and limiting. After all, had I been born Buddhist or Muslim, I would likely have viewed everything from that perspective. As I questioned what made my theological bias true but theirs false, I became aware of The Outsider Test for Faith, a useful device formulated by former evangelical John W. Loftus. This approach encourages individuals of all faiths to assess their truth claims from the perspective of an outsider and with the same level of skepticism they use to evaluate other religious traditions. Applying this methodology to one's own religious perspective can be enlightening and beneficial, though it can be potentially damaging to universal truth claims.

The nineteenth-century Christian existentialist Søren Kierkegaard (1813–1855) famously argued that spiritual truth is neither objective nor certain. Kierkegaard wrote to free people from illusion, and the greatest illusion, he believed, was the view that truth was objective, meaning that one could compress it into creeds or doctrines for all to hold equally and without question. By arguing that truth was subjective, he did not mean to suggest that truth did not exist. However, unlike ethical principles, which can be expressed rationally and categorically, and unlike mathematical principles, which are universally binding yet ultimately impersonal, spiritual truths are by nature passional, subjective, and radically individual. By necessity, such truth is objectively uncertain.

Unlike objective truths, which tend to make us observers, subjective truth makes us participants. Viewed objectively, truth is something humans possess and therefore define. Viewed subjectively, however, truth is something that possesses us and therefore that defines us. For Kierkegaard, religious faith (truth) is not a universal "given" that can be passed on to others or inherited. Such faith is active, not passive, and is paradoxical by nature, for it is characterized by objective uncertainty. Active truth entails "a leap of faith," for it requires trust and commitment before it can be known. To be valid, religious truth must penetrate one's personal existence, for if it does not become one's own, it is meaningless.

Intuitively, we know that Kierkegaard was right, and if truth is essentially subjective, there must be degrees of rightness and wrongness, depending on circumstances and points of view. In our contemporary world, this perspective seems to have much in common with the mindset known as postmodernism, a way of thinking that builds on the assumption that what we call reality is constructed by the mind, and that human understanding is interpretation rather than acquisition of accurate, objective information. From this assumption it follows that knowledge is relative, subjective, and fallible rather than certain and absolute, and that truth is open-ended and inherently ambiguous.

To be clear, I am not denying the validity of facts or particular truths. The realms of science and mathematics rely on probabilities and certainties—on truths—and the realms of ethics and philosophy on absolutes and universals. But when we speak of religious truth, we are in the realm of subjective rather than objective reality.

The Circle and the Ellipse

Most questions religious people ask become hurdles to faith because they are framed incorrectly from the start. The implication behind our questions, the deficiency in our thinking, is that something is true or false, literal or fanciful, revealed or invented, divine or human, particular or universal. The problem with either/or questions is that they promote either/or answers. Such dichotomous forms of thinking set a trap, for the structure of either/or thinking implies that the options presented exhaust all other alternatives: either the Bible is divine or it is human; either one believes there are proofs for God's existence or one is an atheist; if one religion is true, others are false, and so on. Either/or thinking is intolerant of religious pluralism, impatient with both/and resolutions, and dissatisfied with anything less than all-or-nothing answers. It accepts only absolute answers and dismisses uncertainty as a sign of unbelief.

I am fond of the question that has been making the rounds lately: "What is the opposite of faith?" Either/or thinking answers, "Disbelief!" Both/and thinking answers: "Certainty!" The aim of this study guide is to present alternative responses to rigid, either/or approaches that narrow the possibilities for seekers at all stages of their journey.

When I teach a course on Christian theology, I draw an image of a circle and an image of an ellipse, and I explain how an elliptical approach to such concepts as the nature of God, an understanding of sin and salvation, and the relation between faith and reason, provides a more helpful result than approaches that rely on the model of a circle for theological understanding. A circle, of course, has a single center, and everything is determined by its relation to the center. The ellipse, by contrast, is a figure that can be described only in relation to two foci, which cannot be resolved into one.

For example, some people are unable to think elliptically (dialectically) about the question, "Where is God?" so they eliminate the tension between immanence and transcendence by deciding in favor of one polarity, that of supernatural theism—a model that conceptualizes God as "out there" and totally separate from nature. This understanding of God is reductionistic, for it allows for only one correct perspective on the presence of God; if God is "out there," God cannot be "here with us," or vice versa. The symbol of a circle takes us back to "either/or" thinking, a simplistic stance that settles on only one possibly correct answer.

The elliptical model, however, makes it possible to view God as simultaneously transcendent and immanent, for both views are biblical and both are essential to religion. The truth is in the polarity between the two foci, and in the area of overlap; the truth is not one-dimensional but dialectical. When one polarity is emphasized to the detriment or exclusion of the other, religion becomes rigid, intolerant, and increasingly confrontational.

Monovision Rather Than Univision

As I learned recently, while undergoing radiation to reduce the effects of a tumor in my eye, I am one of a small percentage of the human race that has a form of vision known as monovision. The term "monovision" is synonymous with "blended vision," and simply means that one human eye is focused at a different working distance to the other. In the vast majority of monovision cases, one eye—the dominant—is focused for distance vision while the non-dominant eye is focused for near vision. People with monovision enjoy the best of both worlds: adequate distance vision and the ability to read without glasses.

As most people age, their reading vision deteriorates and they have to face the reality of reading glasses. While some people previously required glasses full-time, others face a new reality called presbyopia, putting glasses on and off whenever they need to read. Presbyopia occurs when, as part of the natural aging process, the eye's lens loses its ability to bring close objects into clear focus. For a select number of middle-aged persons, for whom wearing contact lenses or multifocal glasses are helpful but impractical, laser eye surgery increases spectacle independence through the blended vision of monovision. Incidentally, most cataract patients are routinely given a monovision effect so they can maximize their independence from glasses.

To view truth as singular or one-dimensional is like riding a bicycle with only one pedal or like paddling a kayak with only one blade. Two pedals are better than one, two blades better than one. When sailors apply the art of tacking, they use the force of the wind to go against the wind. In judo and other martial arts, this principle enables practitioners to defeat opponents by the force of their own attack. Eastern thought depicts reality by the famous symbol of a circle divided by a reverse S into two equally light and dark areas. This principle, dubbed "complementary dualism" by philosophers or more popularly as "flowing with the Tao," is said to explain the true nature of the universe, which operates on the basis of a balance between opposites: Yin (the negative or passive force in nature) and Yang (the positive or active force in nature). When these two forces are in balance, they complement one another. Neither force is better than the other; both are good and equally necessary. Except for a few objects, such as the sun being yang and the earth being yin, the rest of nature, including healthy individuals, are understood to be a combination of both. When the two forces work together in harmony, life is as it should be.

As two eyes improve one's sight and two legs one's ability to walk, so it is with truth. Like Kierkegaard, I believe that truth is dialectical and dialogical, meaning that it is not primarily cognitive (knowledge-based), outward, static, or certain, but rather relational, inward, discovered, affirmed, dynamic, and tentative. Unlike Kierkegaard, however, I submit that humans arrive at this truth not so much individually but corporately, in dialogue with others (by which I mean not simply through conversation, though that is where it might begin), but by commitment to and with others to the principle that in loving, serving, and respecting others we love and serve God.

Unlike Hegel, who valued a systematic and speculative approach to reality and truth, Kierkegaard launched a counter approach favoring a practical, emotional, and individual approach. In his writings, Kierkegaard alluded to a thesis of the eighteenth-century German Enlightenment thinker G. E. Lessing (1729–1781), that if God held all truth in his right hand, and in his left hand held the lifelong pursuit of it, Lessing would choose the left hand—the pursuit of truth rather than its attainment. Following this approach, we become committed less to goals and results than to the process itself—the dynamic of discovery. And that's what this dialogical approach to essential biblical teachings is designed to accomplish. Tapping into the power of polarities will bring you closer to the synthesis necessary for personal and societal growth: mental and spiritual refinement through the fire of dialogue.

Going Deeper: Reflection for Participants

1. Are you satisfied with your current spiritual state? If so, how do your religious beliefs contribute to your spiritual fulfillment? If not, where are you heading spiritually, and what theological adjustments could you make to get there?

2. John's Gospel has been called "the Gospel of Truth." John 14:6 quotes Jesus as saying that he is the way, the truth, and the life. There are many ways to interpret this statement. What do these words mean to you, and how can you best apply them to the kind of person you need to be? (Hint: If Jesus did say these words, is he asking his followers to relate to him personally or dogmatically?)

3. John 8:32 quotes Jesus as saying that his followers would know the truth, and that through that knowledge, awareness, and commitment they would be set free. In your estimation, what is this truth of which Jesus spoke, and what is the freedom to which he referred?

4. Are ethical principles (the principles of right and wrong) situational and therefore to be applied flexibly and individually by mature adults, or should we consider principles of right and wrong as categorical polarities (opposites) that adults should apply consistently and unfailingly in all situations?

5. In your estimation, what does the author mean when he suggests that truth is dialectical and dialogical rather than systematic and speculative? Do you agree or disagree in principle with this approach? Explain your answer.

6. Assess the value and validity of The Outsider Test for Faith. One of the premises of The Outsider Test for Faith is "that no one religion can lay claim to ultimate truth." Do you agree with this assessment? Support your answer.

7. Kierkegaard argued that truth is essentially subjective. What did he mean? Assess the merits of his perspective. Do you agree or disagree with this approach to truth? Support your answer.

8. Theologians sometimes allude to the circle and the ellipse as models or images for theological understanding. In your estimation, what are the values and limitations of each approach to truth? Which do you prefer? Why?

9. In your estimation, what is the difference between a "monovision" and a "univision" approach to truth? Which do you prefer? Why?

10. In your estimation, what is the primary insight gained from this session?

Session 3

Rethinking Faith

Belief or Trust?

Getting Started

Homework Assignment: Answer the following questions, writing your answers in your journal. Be prepared to share your views with others in the class. 1. Is faith primarily propositional (a dogmatic system of beliefs), relational (and therefore personal and individual), or mystical (a way of living with awe and wonder)? 2. Is faith static, dynamic, or somehow both? Support your answer.

Gaining Momentum

In the previous session we argued the merits of viewing truth dialectically rather than one-dimensionally. When individuals impose or consider specific moral, theological, or doctrinal views to the detriment or exclusion of others, religion becomes rigid, intolerant, and increasingly confrontational. This form of thinking characterizes the religious approach biblical theologian Marcus Borg called the Precritical Paradigm. When polarities are embraced and the truth is sought through dialogue and in the area of overlap, this form of thinking characterizes the religious approach called the Postcritical Paradigm.

Refined by Fire

A Tale of Two Paradigms

It is no secret that we are living in a time of major change, resulting in monumental religious conflict, chiefly in North American mainline denominations. While there are many ways of being Christian in our day, two paradigms—two overarching interpretive frameworks—may be helpful to describe the current conflict in Christianity. The first, the Precritical Paradigm, has been a common form of Christianity for the past several hundred years. This approach should not be associated with Christianity as a whole, though it remains a major voice, perhaps the majority voice in global Christianity. Its adherents

1. View the Bible as a divine product, as the unique revelation of God.
2. Interpret the Bible literally.
3. Equate faith with belief; the Christian life centered in believing now for the sake of salvation.
4. View the afterlife as central; the Christian life being about requirements and rewards, with the main reward a blessed afterlife.
5. View Christianity as the only true religion, and belief in God, the Bible, and Jesus as the way to heaven.

This paradigm should not be equated with "the Christian tradition," as though it were the dominant or only way of being Christian throughout history. In actuality it is the product of modernity, shaped by the birth of modern science and scientific ways of knowing. Since the Enlightenment of the seventeenth century, modernity has questioned both the divine origin and the literal-factual truth of many parts of the Bible, and the Precritical Paradigm is a response to that modern critique.

A second way of seeing Christianity, the Postcritical Paradigm, has been in existence for over a hundred years and has become an increasingly attractive movement within mainline Protestant denominations and in the Catholic Church. Like the earlier paradigm, its central features are a response to the Enlightenment, only in this case it embraces many Enlightenment ideals, including an appreciation of science, historical scholarship, religious pluralism, and cultural diversity. It also arose out of awareness of how Christianity had contributed to racism, sexism, nationalism, exclusivism, and other harmful ideologies. Its adherents

1. View the Bible as a human response to God.

2. Interpret the Bible historically and metaphorically.
3. View faith relationally rather than dogmatically—faith being the way of the heart, not the way of the head.
4. View the Christian life as one of relationship and transformation. Being Christian is not about meeting requirements for a future reward in an afterlife, and not very much about believing. Rather, the Christian life is about a relationship with God that transforms life in the present.
5. Affirm religious pluralism. This paradigm considers Christianity as one of the world's great enduring religions, as a particular response to the experience of God in our Western cultural stream.

From the perspective of the Postcritical Paradigm, the Precritical Paradigm seems anti-intellectual and rigidly (but selectively) moralistic. Its insistence on biblical literalism seems inadequate, as does its rejection of science whenever it conflicts with literalism. It seems to emphasize individual purity more than compassion and justice. And its exclusivism, its rejection of other religions as inadequate or worse, is objectionable. Can it be that God is known in only one religion—and perhaps only in the "right" form of that religion?[1]

The Postcritical Paradigm, guided by the holistic possibilities found in the dialectical model, places equal importance upon faith (as displayed in religious beliefs and practices, both corporate and private) and reason (as displayed in the disciplines of philosophy, science, religious studies, and other academic subjects) in the quest for knowledge and understanding of reality. It also values the antithetical anthropological perspectives suggested in the opening chapters of the book of Genesis—humans are made "in the image of God" in the first creation account (Genesis 1) and "from the dust of the ground" in the second creation account (Genesis 2)—and the tension created by these competing yet harmonizable views. Dialectical thought is simultaneously God-affirming and world-affirming. Advocates of the Postcritical Paradigm need not choose, indeed should not choose, one over the other.

If the transition from a circular to an elliptical model may be said to be characteristic of the Postcritical Paradigm in theology, there is a curious parallel with what occurred in modern astronomy. Until the time of Kepler (1571–1630), it was universally held that the planets moved in

---

1. Borg, *Heart of Christianity*, 16.

circular orbits—this was based not on observation but on the notion that, since the circle was considered to be the perfect figure, God, being perfect, could not have designed the orbits of the planets in any other way. When Kepler discovered that the planets move in elliptical orbits, he changed the shape of the astronomical universe, and, in the process, the course of future theology.

Two Ways of Knowing

Psychologists today recognize up to nine different forms of intelligence, building on a theory of multiple intelligence proposed by Howard Gardner in 1983. The original list included seven cognitive abilities: spatial, linguistic, logical-mathematical, bodily-kinesthetic, musical, interpersonal, and intrapersonal. In 1999 he added another category, which he called "naturalist intelligence," and later suggested yet another, "existential and moral intelligence." This last category is viewed as a spiritual or religious capacity, for it involves the ability to contemplate phenomena or to pursue questions that go beyond sense data.

Just as there are many forms of intelligence, so there are various ways of thinking, speaking, and acquiring knowledge. The ancient Greeks affirmed two modes of thought, calling them *logos* and *mythos*.[2] Both were essential and neither was considered superior to the other. While they were complementary, each having its own sphere of competence, it was considered unwise to mix the two. Both were pragmatic. *Logos* ("reason") helped people organize their societies, control the environment, and invent new technology. Although *logos* was essential to the survival of the species, it had limitations. It could not provide ultimate meaning or help cope with tragedy or with death. For help people turned to *mythos* ("myth").

Today, because we live in a society of scientific *logos*, myth has fallen into disrepute. But in the past, myth, like *logos*, helped people to live effectively in a confusing and uncertain world. Ancient myths have been called a primitive form of psychology, for these stories were therapeutic, designed to help people negotiate the obscure regions of the psyche, areas that influence our thoughts and behavior but are difficult to access. Myths were never intended to be taken literally, as though they were accurate accounts of historical events. A myth was "something that had in some sense

---

2. The material in this segment is adapted from Armstrong, *Case for God*, xi–xiii.

happened once but that also happens all the time."[3] In other words, myths spoke to existential conditions.

A myth would not be effective if someone simply believed in it, for myths were not designed to provide factual information. A myth was essentially a program of action. Although it could put individuals in the correct spiritual or psychological posture, it was up to them to take the next step and make the truth of the myth a reality in their own life. Myths showed people how to live more fully, how to cope with their mortality, and how to embrace life's suffering creatively. If one failed to act upon myth or to apply it to specific situations, it would remain abstract and incredible.

From an early date, myths were enacted in stylized ceremonies (rituals) that worked aesthetically upon participants and, like any work of art, introduced them to a deeper dimension of existence. Myth and ritual were thus inseparable. Without ritual, myths made no sense.

Religion, which builds upon myth (scripture) and ritual (ceremony), was never intended to provide answers that lie within the competence of human reason. That was the role of *logos*. The task of religion was to enable followers to find wisdom, the sort of wisdom that helps them live creatively, peacefully, and even joyously with realities for which there are no easy explanations.

Of course, religion does not work automatically. It is a practical discipline that teaches humans to discover new capacities of mind and heart. Religion, which connects myth with ritual, is not, like *logos*, something that people believe or think, but something people do. Its truth is acquired by practical action, by translating the teachings of religion into ritual or ethical action.

Like any skill, religion requires perseverance, hard work, and discipline. Some people will be better at it than others, some will be inept, and others will miss the point altogether. But those who do not apply themselves will get nowhere at all. Early Daoists, practitioners of one of China's indigenous religious traditions, considered religion as a knack acquired by constant practice. People who acquired this knack discovered a transcendent dimension of life that was not simply an external reality "out there" but was identical with the deepest level of their being. This reality, called by many names and understood in different ways by different religious traditions, has been understood as a fact of human life, though it was impossible to explain solely in terms of *logos*.

3. Ibid., xi.

To counter the dominant influence of *logos* in the development of modern Christianity, we need to become acquainted with a feature in the intellectual and spiritual climate of antiquity known as the apophatic tradition, a mystical approach that flourished during the late patristic and early medieval periods. Subjecting the mind to the heart, apophatic theologians elevated "unknowing" over "knowing," valuing "unknowing" as possibly the most reliable way of understanding what could not be known rationally. This approach, promoted to some extent by theologians such as Origen (185–254), Augustine (354–430) and more fully by Evagrius of Pontus (c. 348–399), Maximus the Confessor (c. 580–662), and Denys the Areopagite (c. 500; late fifth and early sixth centuries), points to the limits of logic and lead us to *apophasis*, the inadequacy of speech, doctrine, and reason, which fragment before the unknowability of God. Preferring emptiness to fullness, darkness to light, silence to speech, faith to reason, and mental stillness to intellectual activity, Christian apophatics (like practitioners of Zen Buddhism) discovered in this "wordless" spirituality the path to peace, union, and inner tranquility. Such a path led not to intellectual ignorance but rather to intellectual rapture, taking its practitioners beyond everyday perceptions and introducing them to another mode of seeing and knowing.

In the contemporary world, this perspective seems to have much in common with the mindset known as postmodernism, a way of thinking that builds on the assumption that what we call reality is constructed by the mind, and that human understanding is interpretation rather than acquisition of accurate, objective information. From this assumption it follows that our knowledge is relative, subjective, and fallible rather than certain and absolute, and that truth is inherently ambiguous.

Four Meanings of Faith[4]

If someone asked you to identify the essence of Christianity, where would you start? Conventional Christians, focusing on dogma, begin with belief in Jesus, the atonement, and the authority of scripture and the church. This approach, however, is antithetical to spirituality. It is a byproduct of the Precritical Paradigm's vision of the Bible and the Christian tradition. Prior to the modern period, faith was not understood in this way. Faith was not about beliefs in one's head but about loyalty, allegiance, and trust in one's heart. Faith, of course, has always been central to Christianity, but an

---

4. The material in this segment is adapted from Borg, *Heart of Christianity*, 28–41.

emphasis on faith as believing difficult things to be true is a relatively recent phenomenon in Christianity, the product of the last few hundred years.

Because religion by nature is primarily experiential, constructing religion on the foundation of belief leads to endless conflict, frustration, and unanswered questions. Children, of course, willingly accept belief, but as they go through adolescence and enter adulthood, many struggle with doubt and disbelief.

Faith, however, makes a better foundation and prepares one more adequately for life. Some readers may wonder about my distinction, because all through life they have equated faith with belief. But faith should not be equated with beliefs. It may reach conclusions about beliefs, but its foundation is experiential and relational rather than doctrinal. Based on experience, faith makes conscious choices that square with that experience.

In the history of Christianity, faith has four primary meanings. The first of these sees faith primarily as a "matter of the head," whereas the remaining three understand faith as a "matter of the heart." Each meaning is described with a Latin term to show its antiquity, as well as how it is understood in English. For each term the opposite is given, for antonyms are often as illuminating as synonyms.

1. Faith as Assent (*assensus*). In this first sense faith means simply "belief," which we take to mean holding a certain set of "beliefs," that is, "believing" certain doctrines or dogmas to be true. This understanding of faith as belief is dominant today, both within the church and outside it. Its dominance in modern Western Christianity is due to the Protestant Reformation, which not only emphasized faith, but also produced numerous denominations, each defining itself by what it "believed," that is, by its distinctive doctrines or confessions.

This development also changed the meaning of the word "orthodoxy." Prior to the Protestant Reformation, orthodoxy referred to "right worship," meaning that those who practiced the liturgy correctly were orthodox. Following the Reformation, orthodoxy began to mean "right belief," and faith began to mean "believing the right things."

The birth of modern science and scientific ways of knowing in the Enlightenment also affected the meaning of "faith" and "believe." When Enlightenment thinkers began identifying truth with factuality, that is, as something verifiable, they began calling into question the reliability of the Bible and of many traditional Christian teachings. As a result, "faith" and "belief" came to be contrasted with knowledge and certainty. For skeptics, faith came to mean "opinion or conviction," something one turned to when knowledge ran out. For believers, faith is what one turned to when beliefs and knowledge conflict.

According to this understanding of faith, the opposite of faith as *assensus* is doubt or disbelief. In its fundamentalist permutation, those who doubt are said to lack faith, whereas those who disbelieve are said to have no faith. While this view is widespread, it puts the emphasis in the wrong place, for it suggests that what God really cares about is the beliefs in our heads, as if having "correct beliefs" is what will save us. As suggested earlier, a better antonym of faith is certainty.

Faith starts with the willingness to recognize and question the core mysteries at the heart of existence: why we exist at all and how to make meaning out of our existence. As a result, it puts on our radar the yearning for the answers to these ultimate questions and the consequent intuition that draws us to the words, ideas, and rituals of the religious tradition that attempts to answer them. We cannot know the answers to the ultimate questions as we can know scientific answers, which build bodies of knowledge over time. Religious answers are more like wisdom. Often they are paradoxical. Sometimes they require us to examine things backward: to increase by diminishing, to multiply by dividing, to hold on by letting go. With the habit of faith, we are willing to ponder such questions in our hearts and minds. Quoting Augustine, Aquinas says that belief is "giving assent to something one is still thinking about."

We turn now to the meanings of faith that are relational, those having more to do with the heart.

2. Faith as Trust (*fiducia*). In its second and higher sense, faith means "trust" in something or someone. In the Bible, it means radical trust in God. Significantly, it does not mean trusting in the truth of a set of statements about God, for that would simply be *assensus* under a different name. While our behavior is important, God seems to be less concerned with our actions than with our character, for our actions flow from our will: "For the Lord does not see as mortals see; they look on the outward appearance, but the Lord looks on the heart" (1 Sam. 16:7).

Faith is like floating in a deep ocean. If you struggle, if you tense up and thrash about, you will eventually sink. But if you relax and trust, you will float. Like the story of Peter walking on the water with Jesus, when he began to be afraid, he began to sink. According to this meaning, the opposite of *fiducia* is not doubt or disbelief, but mistrust, which results in worry and anxiety. Four times in the extended passage from Matthew's Sermon on the Mount, Jesus says to his hearers, "Do not worry," and then adds, "You of little faith" (Matt. 6:25–34). Lack of trust and anxiety go together; if you are anxious, you have little faith.

3. Faith as Faithfulness (*fidelitas*). In the Bible, faith is the trustful acceptance of God's promises, particularly of God's desire to bless all peoples and nations of the world. But faith is also trust in God's faithfulness to the promise, that is, in God's ability to deliver Good News to everyone, something that God accomplishes through Jesus Christ and his followers. Because God is steadfast and faithful, we too are called to faithfulness. *Fidelitas* does not mean faithfulness to beliefs about God, whether biblical, creedal, or doctrinal. Rather it refers to radical centering in the God to whom the Bible and creeds and doctrines point.

The English equivalent to *fidelitas* is "fidelity." Faith as fidelity means loyalty, allegiance, the commitment of the self at its deepest level. Its opposite is not doubt or disbelief. Rather, as in human relationships, its opposite is infidelity, being unfaithful to our relationship with God. To use a striking biblical metaphor, the opposite of this meaning of faith is adultery. Another vivid biblical term for infidelity to God is idolatry, meaning not so much the worship of idols as false gods, but centering in something finite rather than the sacred, which is infinite and beyond all images. As the opposite of idolatry, faith means being loyal to God "and not to the seductive would-be lords of our lives," whether one's nation, affluence, achievement, family, or desire.[5]

In the Hebrew Bible, faith as fidelity is the meaning of the first of the Ten Commandments: "You shall have no other gods before me." In the New Testament, it is the meaning of the Great Commandment: "You shall love the Lord your God with all your heart, soul, mind, and strength." This commandment is followed immediately by the exhortation to "love your neighbor as yourself." *Fidelitas* means being faithful to these two great relationships: God and your neighbor. And one's neighbor, as Jesus explains in the parable of the Good Samaritan, is first and foremost the person who is in need of help (Luke 10:29–37).

One is faithful to God, therefore, by being attentive to these two primary relationships. We are attentive to God through worship, prayer, and practice, and faithful to our neighbor through a life of compassion

---

5. Ibid., 33.

and justice. To be faithful to God also means to love that which God loves, which includes the whole of creation.

4. Faith as Vision (*visio*). As the English word "vision" suggests, faith is a way of seeing reality, and how we view the whole affects how we respond to life. There are basically three ways we can see the whole:

- We can see reality as *hostile and threatening*, and therefore respond to life defensively, doing whatever we can to survive, for that is all that matters. Many forms of popular religion have viewed reality this way: God (or Life, or Nature) is going to get us, unless we behave the right way, practice the correct rituals, offer the right sacrifices, or believe the right things;.

- We can see reality as *indifferent* to human purposes and ends. Although this response to life will be less anxious than that of the first way, we are still likely to be defensive and precautionary. We respond by building up whatever security we can, even enjoying and seeking to take care of the world, but ultimately we are likely to be concerned primarily for ourselves and those who are most important to us.

- We can see reality as *life-giving, nourishing, and full of promise*. To use a traditional theological term, to see reality as filled with wonder and beauty, and to nourish and spread this goodness, leads to radical trust. It frees us from the anxiety, self-preoccupation, and concern to protect the self with systems of security that mark the first two viewpoints. It leads to the ability to love and to be present to the moment. It generates a commitment to spend oneself for the sake of a vision that extends beyond ourselves. To use Paul's words, it leads to a life marked by the "fruit of the Spirit": love, joy, peace, patience, kindness, generosity, faithfulness, gentleness, and self-control" (Gal. 5:22–23). These qualities are the result of a way of life that Paul characterizes as "freedom" (Gal. 5:1); freedom *from* evil and from allegiance to false authorities; freedom *for* love. For Paul, faith becomes active "through love" (Gal. 5:6).

To understanding faith as *visio* is to see reality as gracious; its opposite, un-faith, views reality as hostile and indifferent. This meaning of faith is closely related to *fiducia*, to faith as trust. Trust and vision go together; trust in God—the God of promise and faithfulness—and how we view God go together. In this way of life, radical centering in God leads to a deepening trust that transforms the way we view reality and live our lives. Seeing, living, trusting, and centering are all related in complex and salutary ways.

As we have noted, faith is relational, but this does not mean that beliefs don't matter. There are affirmations that are central to the Christian faith, affirmations such as the reality of God, the centrality of Jesus, and the significance of the Bible. These beliefs are essential, not only for Christians, but for people of all faiths, when properly understood. Faith as a way of seeing at the deepest level requires avoiding the human tendency toward excessive precision and certitude. Christian theology has often been plagued by both—the desire to know too much and to know it too precisely. Our minds tell us that such knowledge is not possible—perhaps not even desirable—and people cannot easily give their heart to something that their mind rejects. Properly understood, a deep but humble understanding of Christian faith as *assensus* is close to faith as *visio*. As we have seen, biblical and theological faith need not be viewed as assent to narrow propositions or as fulfilling specific requirements, but as a persuasive and compelling way of seeing reality.

While faith involves the mind, faith is primarily the way of the heart. Given the premodern meaning of "believe," to believe in God is to love God and to love that which God loves. The Christian life is as simple and challenging as that.

Going Deeper: Reflection for Participants

1. Which traditional Christian beliefs do you question or need to rethink?
2. What role should doubt play in the Christian life?
3. In your understanding, are "faith" and "belief" essentially similar or dissimilar concepts? Should our theological beliefs change or adjust as we mature emotionally and intellectually? Should our faith remain constant through life or must it change as well?
4. Which paradigm do you find most attractive, the Precritical or the Postcritical? Support your answer.
5. If you are a Christian, do you consider yourself an exclusivist, an inclusivist, a pluralist, or something else? Support your answer.

6. Scholars suggest that religions consist of "myth and ritual." What do they mean by "myth" and what roles does mythology play in humanity's search for meaning? Are all religions ultimately mythological in nature?
7. This chapter presented four definitions of faith. Which do you find most compelling? Why?
8. If faith is related to the intellect, what is the first step in the renewal of one's mind?
9. In your own words, explain the role of faith in spiritual transformation.
10. In your estimation, what is the primary insight gained from this session?

Session 4

Rethinking God (the Sacred)
Personal or Transpersonal?

Getting Started

Homework Assignment: Answer the following questions, writing your answers in your journal. Be prepared to share your views with others in the class. 1. Is deity personal, impersonal, or transpersonal (beyond personality)? 2. Is deity immanent, transcendent, or somehow both? Support your answer.

Gaining Momentum

One of the benefits of being a college professor is that summers become mini-sabbaticals. They provide opportunities to rethink views, create courses, and update syllabi. Consequently, during my teaching career I was able to create forty new courses and seminars, many of them developed at Chautauqua Institution in upstate New York, where I met world-class theologians and listened to some of America's most innovative thinkers.

At Chautauqua I heard lectures by cutting-edge scholar Karen Armstrong and "Jesus scholars" Marcus Borg and John Dominic Crossan. I purchased their books and read them thoroughly, incorporating some of their ideas into my lectures. I also read books on comparative religions and grappled with John Hick's notion of "religious pluralism" and Brian

McLaren's concepts of "a new kind of Christian" and "a generous orthodoxy." Although these writers tilled the soil of my spirit and sowed transformative seeds, none prompted the wake-up call that I experienced during the first week of the 2010 Chautauqua season, when I attended a weeklong series of lectures delivered by Bishop John Shelby Spong, who was promoting his new book *Eternal Life: A New Vision*.

For that series of talks, which included a panel discussion and five public lectures, a crowd of over one thousand people gathered to listen, to question, and to interact with key concepts from Spong's writings. In keeping with my customary response to such presentations, I took copious notes, purchasing and then reading several of the speaker's books. During the ensuing academic year, while transcribing notes from that experience, I recognized the effect cosmic and human evolution had upon Spong's theology, and my outlook changed dramatically. Shortly thereafter, I accepted the evolutionary teachings of Charles Darwin as foundational for my worldview. That decision forced me to reexamine my belief system and its assumptions. Of these, perhaps the most important conclusion was the inadequacy of supernatural theism, a topic discussed in my 2012 volume on faith, science, and reason titled *Beyond Belief*. In my estimation, the moral, logical, and spiritual problems regarding theistic supernaturalism (the traditional view of God as all-powerful and supreme ruler of the universe) are so formidable that they leave modern, educated persons with three options: ignorance, atheism, or an alternative view of God.

A person's view of God is vital because it serves as a lens through which people view reality, influencing their perspective of life, the cosmos, others, and of themselves. As one's view of self provides a microcosm of reality, so one's view of God serves as a macrocosm of that reality. If one's view of God is positive—such as lover or friend—then the universe seems benevolent, others are valued, and the self is considered good. However, if one's view of God is negative—such as angry antagonist or vindictive judge—then the universe seems harsh, others are devalued, and the self is considered evil or sinful.

Theology is "talk about God." The majority of people who use the term "God," particularly in the Western world, have in mind a theistic concept of God, meaning an all-powerful and supreme ruler of the universe. Supernatural theism, by implication, includes the view that all finite things are dependent in some way on this ultimate reality, a reality generally described in personal terms. After all, imaging God as a personal being is very common in the Bible. It is also the natural language of worship and prayer, and there is nothing wrong with it in such contexts. A transcendent reality that does not possess at the very least those qualities that constitute the dignity of human beings, qualities such as intelligence, feeling, freedom, power, initiative, and creativity, could not adequately inspire trust or reverence in human beings. In this sense, God would have to be "personal" to be God. It is doubtful whether believers could worship something that does not have at least the stature of personality.

While the idea of a "personal God" is beneficial in that it makes God relational and accessible to humanity, the extremes of this position, such as presented in the Hebrew scriptures, raise insuperable problems for people in the modern era. This God fights wars and defeats enemies, chooses people and works through them, sends storms, heals the sick, spares the dying, rewards goodness, and punishes evil. Many people have trouble intellectually with these anthropomorphic renderings of God and with the seeming irrationality of belief in a personal God. While only the most traditional believers and the most literal readers of scripture believe such things anymore, this deity remains the primary object and substance of the Christian church's faith. It is this understanding of God that is becoming meaningless to increasing numbers in the modern world.

While it is attractive to speak of intimacy with God and accessibility to God, religious philosophers have long warned against ascribing human qualities and attributing human feelings to God. Still, the joy of familiarity with God and the need to recognize and be recognized by God override the philosopher's critique. There is, however, a critical flaw in this perspective: Once we conceive of God as a person like ourselves, God becomes open to criticism.

To protect God, apologists and theologians urge us to discard this way of thinking. God is not like us, says twentieth-century theologian Karl Barth; God is "Totally Other." This understanding views God as different not only in degree but also in kind. Humans can only speak of God indirectly, says thirteenth-century theologian Thomas Aquinas, for they cannot "know" God directly. Humans can only speak of God or "know" God indirectly, by saying what God is not (the *via negativa*), or by saying what God is like, thereby resorting to analogies or metaphors (the *via analogia*).

In using models of transcendence, whereby God is said to be all knowing, all powerful, and all good, we instinctively know that we are not referring to the same kind of qualities we understand when speaking of attributes in humans. Does this mean, then, that God cannot be said to be moral in the manner that we are said to be moral? If so, that raises deep resentments. We hear it in the outburst of the philosopher John Stuart Mill: "I will call no being good who is not what I mean when I apply the epithet to my fellow creatures, and if such a being can sentence me to hell, to hell I will go."[1] In his publication, *The Sins of Scripture*, Bishop Spong examines biblical moral principles attributed to the will of God and concludes that those who wish to base their morality literally on the Bible have either not read it or not understood it.

As Rabbi Harold Schulweis observes, "In elevating God to the level of transcendent lawgiver and judge, the human being is drawn increasingly subordinate to the will of God. An alienating dualism has intruded in the original picture, splitting the divine and the human, erecting a wall between God 'above' and nature 'below.' As a result, questions about prayer, miracles, and revelation are turned into forced either/or options. Prayer is either a unilateral response from God or a lonely human monologue; miracle is either God's intervention or human invention; revelation is either God's word cast down from above or a soliloquy from below."[2]

Bishop Spong spoke forcefully and shockingly when he wrote:

> There is no supernatural God who lives above the sky or beyond the universe. There is no supernatural God who can be understood as animating spirit, Earth Mother, masculine tribal deity or external monotheistic being. There is no parental deity watching over us from whom we can expect help. There is no deity whom we can flatter into acting favorably or manipulate by being good. There are no record books and no heavenly judge keeping them to serve as the basis on which human beings will be rewarded or punished. There is also no way that life can be made to be fair or that a divine figure can be blamed for its unfairness. Heaven and hell are human constructs designed to make fair in some ultimate way the unfairness of life. The idea that in an afterlife the unfairness of this world will be rectified is a pious dream, a toe dip into unreality. Life is lived at the whim of luck and chance, and no one can earn the good fortune of luck and chance.[3]

With Spong, I too recoil at these words, for the traditional understanding of God has been my guide from the beginning. Unlike some who

---

1. Cited by Schulweis, *Those Who Can't Believe*, 132.
2. Ibid.
3. Spong, *Eternal Life*, 121–22.

Rethinking God (the Sacred)

have concluded that God is no more, Spong does not mean to say that God once existed but has since died. Nor does he mean to say that there is no God. What he calls "God" is real, only not as popularly conceived.[4]

But what are the alternatives? Is atheism (a-theism) the only alternative to theism? Technically, of course, there are numerous options, including polytheism (the belief that there are numerous deities), pantheism (the belief that God is in everything for everything is divine), henotheism (the notion of worshipping a territorial god, conceived as one god among many), animism (the belief that nature is filled with spirits or souls, which must be worshipped or appeased), and panentheism.

Many people today are finding the case for panentheism increasingly attractive in an age of science and reason. One can find historical traces of panentheism in both western and eastern orthodox theology, though the word itself was popularized by English philosopher Alfred North Whitehead (1861–1947). Panentheism is not the same as pantheism, the concept that "all things are God." Rather, panentheism is the concept that "all things are *in* God." Panentheism views God not as a supernatural being separate from the universe, beyond nature and history, but as the encompassing Spirit around us and within us. According to this conception, God is more than the universe, yet the universe is in God. Viewed spatially, God is not "out there" but "right here." Whereas supernatural theism emphasizes God's transcendence—God's otherness, God as more than the universe—panentheism affirms both the transcendence and immanence of God. It does not deny or subordinate one in order to affirm the other. For panentheism, God is both more than the universe and yet everywhere present in the universe.

In this regard, panentheism is located between traditional theism and pantheism. As David Ray Griffin describes it, panentheism "combines features of both pantheism, which regards God as 'essentially immanent and in no way transcendent,' and traditional theism, which regards God 'as essentially transcendent and only accidentally immanent.'"[5] Griffin's work helps to explain why panentheism isn't just pantheism with a new name: "Panentheism is crucially different from pantheism because God tran-

---

4. The conventional understanding of God, based in part on medieval debates and the language of certain classical theologians, attributes to deity such qualities as impassibility (that God cannot experience pain and suffering), transcendence (that God is eternal and unchanging and largely unrelated to this world), and omnipotence (unlimited in power and capable of doing all things). Overall, such views are unbiblical and, with regard to the concept of "omnipotence," philosophically indefensible.

5. Griffin, *Reenchantment*, 141.

scends the universe in the sense that God has God's own creative power, distinct from that of the universe of finite actualities. Hence, each finite actual entity has its own creativity with which to exercise some degree of self-determination, so that it transcends the divine influence upon it."[6]

Theologians in various traditions have offered different ways of defining and modeling this God-world relationship. According to the influential German evangelical theologian Jürgen Moltmann, in the panentheistic view God, having created the world, also dwells in it, and conversely the world which he has created exists in him. He writes of God "making space," a *nothing* (*nihil*) to which God gives being (*creatio ex nihilo*). "God does not create merely by calling something into existence . . . In a more profound sense he 'creates' by letting-be, by making room, by withdrawing himself."[7] Moltmann's language expresses the idea of the world, including humanity, as "enveloped by God without losing its true distinctiveness."[8] Consonant with Moltmann's theology, Anglican theologian Arthur Peacocke writes that "God is best conceived of as the circumambient [i.e., surrounding] reality enclosing all existing entities, structures and processes, and as operating in and through all, while being 'more' than all. Hence, all that is not God has its existence within God's operation and Being." Other panentheistic models have been suggested, but all reveal a common theme: the world is given existence, energy, life, nourishment, and continuous creation by the God in whom "we live and move and have our being" (Acts 17:28).

Fortunately there are alternatives to the concept of theism, for "theism" and "God" need not be the same. Supernatural theism is but one human definition of God. Panentheists affirm that "God" does not refer to a supernatural being "in heaven," apart from nature, but rather to the sacred at the center of existence, the holy mystery that is around us and within us. Panentheism affirms the centrality of mystery in the universe and the possibility of relating intellectually and experientially to that mystery. It is possible, then, to be an agnostic or even an atheist regarding the God of supernatural theism and yet be a believer in God in the way offered by panentheism.

One of the most persistent aspects of the "problem of God" is that there is no unambiguous evidence in our ordinary experience of any providential, transcendent, divine presence. Many atheists and agnostics point

---

6. Ibid., 142.
7. Moltmann, *God in Creation*, 88–89.
8. Clayton and Peacocke, *In Whom We Live*, 145.

to this and wonder how truly intelligent persons can be believers. But the point here is that the reality of God is no less capable of immediate validation than are the dimensions of depth, future, freedom, beauty, and truth. For God not to be accessible to our senses or our wishes should be no more outrageous than that these dimensions are incapable of being brought under our comprehending control. God is not one object among others in our experience. Rather, God may be understood as the ultimate horizon that makes all experience possible in the first place. The sacred does not force itself into the range of objects or events that make up the content of ordinary experience. Instead, God may be viewed as the inexhaustible depth and ground out of which all our experiences arise.

Whitehead, whose philosophy is permeated by aesthetic considerations, has shown that an unduly narrow doctrine of perception, limited to the five senses, has dominated much of modern thought. Without denying that our senses do connect us with the real world, Whitehead emphasizes that the senses are inadequate to mediate the full complexity of the world, giving us only an abstract and narrow range of the universe. By distinguishing between the sharply defined region of sense data and the vaguer but deeper organic perception that lies beneath sensation, he provides a doctrine of perception that allows us to understand the "absence of God." God is necessarily hidden from the realm of sense objects simply because sense perception is too narrow to give us the deeper and more important aspects of reality. Furthermore, possessing something—comprehending God—eliminates the longing for it. The paradox of suspension between having and not having, knowing and not knowing, is the very condition that makes it possible for us to ask questions and to seek the truth. Religion, then, may be understood as the conscious rejection of the strong temptation to make truth—understood rationally and cognitively—the object of our mastery. It is a surrender to truth as the *mysterium tremendum et fascinars* in which alone our freedom and fulfillment lie. Wherever there is a sincere desire for the truth about ourselves, others, and the world there is authentic religion, even if it does not go by that name.

Whitehead encourages us to accept the "absence of God" as the necessary condition for the aesthetic intensity and significance of our lives. The name he gives to this ongoing quest is *adventure*. This is religion, in its pure, undistorted essence: religion is adventure. The universe that we inhabit may itself be understood—and science supports this position—as an adventure. It appears to be a fifteen or twenty billion-year-old quest for more and more intense forms of ordered novelty ... Religion must be seen as continuous with the universe's risk-filled episodes of adventure. Otherwise, it is unrelated to the rest of reality.

Organized religions, insofar as they have allied with the status quo, with predictability and monotony, have displayed a keen antipathy toward adventure. Because they teach a doctrine of ultimate order, their teachings are easily perverted into divine sanctions for particular socio-political order. As such, religion feeds on our fear of adventure, losing its vitality whenever it forfeits the risk required by openness to novelty. A purely conservative religion, while manifesting an understandable passion for order, promotes the stagnation of monotony and the suspension of life's narrative story.

At its normative best, religion has provided the most adventurous component in the historical evolution of human consciousness. Its openness to novelty and the risk involved in this openness are evidenced in its great religious innovators and visionaries. In attempting to implant their vision, they and their followers have inevitably disturbed the monotony of the status quo. A truly adventurous religious spirit will always disrupt the cult of monotony while at the same time promising hope.

In his accessible book titled *The God We Never Knew* (1998), biblical scholar Marcus Borg examined the variety of images of God in the biblical and Christian traditions and discerned therein two primary "models":

1. The "*monarchical model*," which clusters images of God as king, lord, and father. This approach leads to what Borg calls a "performance model" of the Christian life.

2. The "*Spirit model*," which clusters images of God that point to intimate relationship and belonging. This model leads to a "relational model" of the Christian life.

Both models, Borg discovered, are found throughout all periods of Christian history, though the first is more common. From roughly the fourth century—when Christianity became the dominant religion of Western culture—through the present, the monarchical model has dominated. But alongside it, as an alternative voice, the Spirit model has also persisted. These models reflect two different voices within the Christian tradition.

The monarchical model portrays God as male, as all-powerful, as lawgiver, and as judge. Images of God in this model suggest that God is distant. Within this model, humans have offended divine majesty and deserve judgment. But because God loves his subjects, God creates a way for his people to escape the punishment they deserve: through appropriate sacrifice and true repentance. In the royal theology of ancient Israel, atonement was institutionalized in temple rituals. In the Christian version of the monarchical model, the king's (Lord's) love is seen especially in Jesus. Because God loves us, he sends his son into the world to die on a cross as the sacrifice that makes our forgiveness possible.[9]

The Spirit model, as used in the Bible, is broader than the specific Christian doctrine of "the Holy Spirit," which sees the Spirit as one aspect of God. In the Bible, Spirit is used comprehensively to refer to God's presence in creation, in the history of Israel, and in the life of Jesus and the early church. While the monarchical model also affirms that God is Spirit, of course, and that affirmation can be a source of confusion that limits our understanding of God, there is a difference. When Spirit is assimilated to the monarchical model, God is not Spirit but a spirit—that is, a spiritual being out there, not here. But when Spirit is set free from the monarchical understanding, Spirit retains the suggestive meanings associated with breath and wind: God is the encompassing Spirit both within and outside us.[10]

In addition to wind and breath, the Bible provides other non-anthropomorphic images, such as rock (meaning a place of refuge and safety). Additional non-masculine images include mother, wisdom, lover, and shepherd. These metaphors for the Spirit affect our root image of God in quite obvious ways: (1) they emphasize *the nearness of God* rather than the distance implied by the monarchical model, thereby suggesting the language of relationship; (2) they utilize *both male and female metaphors* (as well as some that are neuter), rather than the exclusively male images of the monarchical model; and (3) they include *both anthropomorphic and nonathropomorphic images*. Taken together, both models suggest that the relationship to God is personal, even as God is more than a person. The sacred is not simply an inanimate mystery but a presence. Using an ancient biblical analogy, these metaphors lead to a covenantal understanding of the divine-human relationship, which emphasizes belonging and connectedness. This model is intrinsically dialogical.[11]

---

9. Borg, *God We Never Knew*, 63–64.
10. Ibid., 72.
11. Ibid., 75–76.

The Spirit model of God affects the meaning of a number of central Christian teachings. It does so by changing the framework in which things are seen. Borg provides four examples:

1. *Creation looks different.* According to the monarchical model, God's creation of the world is understood as an event in the distant past involving the creation of a universe separate from God. The Spirit model depicts God's creation as an ongoing activity: in every moment God as Spirit (as the nonmaterial "ground" of all that is) is bringing the universe into existence.

2. *The human condition looks different.* Our central problem is not sin and guilt, as it is within the monarchical model, but "estrangement," meaning that humans are separated from that to which they belong. Our problem is blindness to the presence of God, separation from the Spirit that is all around us and within us and to which we belong.

3. *Sin looks different.* For the monarchical model, sin is primarily disloyalty to the king, seen especially as disobedience to his laws. The Spirit model addresses "sin" is more profound ways: for the metaphor of God as lover, sin is unfaithfulness; for the metaphor of God as the compassionate one who cares for all her children, sin is failure in compassion. Thus sin remains, but as betrayal of relationship and absence of compassion. Repentance also remains, only now it does not require sacrifice and contrition but a turning and returning to that to which we belong. Judgment also remains, only now not as the threat of eternal judgment but rather as living with the consequences of our choices. To remain estranged from God is to remain unsatisfied and unfulfilled.

4. *God as king and lord looks different.* God as Spirit is glorious, radiant, and splendid, like the splendor of a king. In the Spirit model, God as king and lord is the subverter of systems of domination, not the legitimator of domination systems.[12]

The images of God associated with the Spirit model dramatically affect how we think of the Christian life. Rather than God as a distant being with whom we might spend eternity, Spirit—the sacred—is right here. Rather than sin and guilt being the central dynamic of the Christian life, the central dynamic becomes relationship—with God, the world, and each other.

12. Ibid., 77–78.

Rethinking God (the Sacred)

The mystics of every religious tradition, following the Spirit model rather than the monarchical model, have always spoken out against specific definitions of God. The Western mystics appear to have assumed that a personal God was only a stage, and an inferior one at that, in human religious development. The mystical portrait of God was first imaginative, and then ineffable. It involved an interior journey, not an exterior one. In the mystical tradition no one can claim objectivity for his or her insight. Each person is called to journey into the mystery of God along the pathway of his or her own expanding personhood. Every person is thus capable of being a theophany, as sign of God's presence; but no one person, institution, or way of life can exhaust this revelation. God, for the mystics, is found at the depths of life, working in and through the being of this world, calling all nature to its deepest potential.

Alfred North Whitehead, who began his professional life as a mathematician, laid out the theological framework for perceiving God not as a divine being external to the universe, but as a divine process coming into being within the life of this world. This conception of God as existing with all of reality, not prior to it, became known as process theology. Dietrich Bonhoeffer called the world to something he named "religionless Christianity," suggesting in his letters, written from prison as he awaited his execution by the Third Reich, that Christians need to live in this world "as if there were no God." His death as a martyr prevented him from conceptualizing further the implications of his hypothesis, but a religionless—perhaps even a nontheistic or godless—Christianity appeared on the horizon of his thinking.

Paul Tillich, himself a refugee from Nazi Germany, proposed as far back as the 1930s and 1940s that Western Christians should abandon the external height images in which the theistic God had historically been perceived, replacing them with internal depth images of a deity not apart from us but the very core and ground of all that is. This God was not a person, but rather was the mystical presence in which all personhood could flourish. This God was not a being but rather the power that called being forth in all creatures. This God was not an external, personal force that could be invoked but rather an internal reality that, when confronted, opened us to the meaning of life itself.[13] Tillich, who believed that the word "God" had been distorted by the inadequate images of the past, was convinced that those images must die before the word "God" could ever be used again with

---

13. Spong, *Christianity Must Change*, 64.

meaning. He urged a moratorium on the use of the word "God" for at least a hundred years.

Following Tillich, Bishop Spong provides a model that integrates the Christian doctrine of the Trinity with this understanding of God. The meaning of God, according to his conception, is understood as (1) the source of life, (2) the source of love, and (3) the ground of being. He finds in this triune understanding a portrait of God embodied in Jesus of Nazareth, a whole human being who lived fully, who loved lavishly, and who had the courage to be himself under every circumstance.

So the call of this internal God found in our depths becomes primarily a call into being, a call that is not unique to religion. It is a call that refocuses what has been known as the religious dimension. In this scenario, the task of the church becomes less that of indoctrinating or relating people to an external divine power and more that of providing opportunities for people to touch the infinite center of all things and to fulfill all their potential. This understanding of God places a premium on the church's vocation to oppose anything that prevents us from the fullest expression of our humanity.

We are learning that "meaning" is not external to life but must be discovered in our own depths and imposed on life by an act of our own will. We are being made aware that life is not fair and will not necessarily be made fair either in this life or in any other. So we have to decide how we will live now with this reality. One thing is certain: the journey of faith must go forward.

Years ago, J. B. Phillips, translator of the celebrated *New Testament in Modern English* (1958), wrote a small volume titled *Your God is Too Small*. If, in describing our understanding of God, we are found to be heterodox, I trust it will be because our God is too big rather than too small. If our views differ from the mainstream of current Christian orthodoxy, we may find that they belong to that tradition of Christian orthodoxy described in Session 2 as apophatic,[14] rather than in the prevalent Western theological tradition characterized as kataphatic.[15]

---

14. The term "apophatic" refers to ways of knowing God that are direct and not mediated. Apophatics reflect an intuitive form of spirituality, which views God as ineffable and indescribable. Apophatics are comfortable with ambiguity and, when speaking of God, they prefer terms such as Mystery or Spirit. They prefer to worship God in silence or by striving for justice and peace in the world.

15. The term "kataphatic" refers to ways of knowing God that are indirect and mediated. Kataphatics reflect a sensate form of spirituality, which prefers concrete images of God. Kataphatics are often divided into two groups: those who prefer to worship verbally

Rethinking God (the Sacred)

Going Deeper: Reflection for Participants

1. Do you agree with the statement that one's view of God serves as a lens by which one views life, the cosmos, others, and oneself? Support your answer.

2. Can people worship God or even relate to God meaningfully apart from a "personal" (theistic) understanding of God? Explain your answer.

3. What, in your experience, is the greatest evidence and therefore the greatest attractiveness of the traditional view of a providential, transcendent, divine being? What is the greatest deterrent to such a view?

4. Medieval theologian Thomas Aquinas argued that there are only two ways to know God, that is, to speak of God. What did he mean by that? Assess the merits of his perspective.

5. In *The Sins of Scripture*, Bishop Spong argued that those who wish to base their morality literally on the Bible have either not read it or not understood it. In your estimation, which portions of scripture did he have in mind?

6. In *Eternal Life*, Bishop Spong argued against the existence of a supernatural deity living in heaven. What did he mean by that statement? Assess the merits of his perspective. Do you agree or disagree with his approach? Support your answer.

7. In a few sentences, define panentheism. How does this view differ from theism? Why is this approach to God becoming increasingly attractive to people today? Assess the merits of this perspective.

8. Which of Borg's two biblical models for God do you find most attractive, the "monarchical" or the "spirit" model? Must we choose between them? Is there a better model?

9. Assess Spong's triune approach to God, Jesus, and the Spirit as (a) the source of life, (b) the source of love, and (c) the ground of being. Describe the "growing edge" in your understanding of God.

10. Using J. B. Phillips's analogy, is your current view of God "too small," "too big," or "just right"?

---

and sacramentally and those who prefer to worship spontaneously and whole-heartedly, with the senses and the emotions.

11. In your estimation, what is the primary insight gained from this session?

Session 5

Rethinking Jesus
Preexistent Lord or Palestinian Jew?

Getting Started

Homework Assignment: Answer the following question, writing your answer in your journal. Be prepared to share your views with others in the class. 1. In our understanding of Jesus, should we focus on his humanity and historicity (Christology "from below"), on his preexistence and deity (Christology "from above"), or on both simultaneously? Explain your answer, addressing the pitfalls or limitations associated with each view.

Gaining Momentum

The central theme of the New Testament is a person, Jesus of Nazareth, a wandering preacher of the first century who has changed the course of history. Whether Christian or not, all who live in the Western world have been influenced by the teachings and life of this individual. Early disciples envisioned Jesus as the climactic historical figure, the Messiah who brought the long-awaited messianic kingdom of God, a rule that by ending evil and suffering would usher in an age of bliss. Later followers and even unbelievers would view Jesus' historical role as pivotal, representing its midpoint. Ernst Renan, famous nineteenth-century scholar, maintained this view when he wrote: "All history is incomprehensible without Christ"; also Napoleon, who confessed toward the end of his life: "This man, Jesus, vanished for eighteen hundred years, still holds the character of men as in a vise"; and H. G. Wells, who once declared: "I am an historian. I am not a believer. But I must confess, as an historian, that this penniless preacher from Galilee is irresistibly the center of history."

The message of the New Testament is reducible to two claims: (1) that Jesus' appearance and career came at the climax of a series of historical events of which the Old Testament is witness, and (2) that God was in Christ, confronting humanity with reconciling power and transforming truth. The paradoxical emphasis upon both Jesus' humanity and deity is evident not just in his message but in his life, his actions, and his person.

Understanding Jesus through Jewish Eyes

The whole of the New Testament—every book, chapter, and verse—is theology: all is written from faith for faith (Rom. 1:17), by believers for the edification of other believers, or for the conviction of unbelievers, that they might be brought to faith. All twenty-seven books are written to explain and promote faith in Jesus Christ.

Biblical scholars famously distinguish between the "Jesus of history" and the "Christ of faith." While the New Testament writers spoke eloquently about the latter, what did they say about the former? Who was Jesus of Nazareth?

Although we cannot be precise about the length of his life or even the duration of his ministry, scholars maintain that Jesus was born around 5 BC, shortly before the death of Herod in 4 BC, and that he died by crucifixion around AD 30. The New Testament is a response to Jesus of Nazareth, whom Christians call Christ, and to a cluster of events scholars call the "Christ event," centered on his birth, death, and resurrection.

Like other great religious teachers, Jesus left nothing in writing. While he may have been familiar with some Greek words, throughout his ministry he seems to have spoken Aramaic, a form of Semitic speech akin to Hebrew and Syriac that became a lingua franca over a large part of the Middle East. This means that every saying attributed to him in the Greek New Testament has come to us through translation. Even his teachings and the traditions concerning Jesus were passed on orally, so little, if anything, was written down. During the oral period (AD 30–50, the years between the date of the crucifixion and the first letter written by Paul), the sayings of Jesus circulated mostly as isolated units, detached from their original context, and preserved in connection with the preaching and teaching activities of early Christians. The famous missionary doctor Albert Schweitzer, at the end of his survey of scholarly attempts to write the life of Jesus, concluded that such a task cannot be accomplished: "He comes to us as One unknown, without a name, as of old by the lake-side He came to those who knew Him not."[1] Jesus, he declared, could only be known by faith. Many current biblical scholars are less pessimistic, recognizing that in the Gospels, particularly in the Synoptic Gospels, there is a great deal of material that can be accepted as genuinely historical and therefore as going back to Jesus himself.

It is clear that the human Jesus must have been a figure of great power and originality. In him a force of immeasurable magnitude began to operate in this world, unleashing a movement that has lasted through twenty centuries and is yet on the rise globally. When a person of such eminence appears, who can apprehend that person totally? One observer will see one aspect, another a different aspect; and even the collection of their observations cannot yield the whole person. Of course, no one can know another person completely. Even after years of marriage, husbands and wives often discover aspects of one another's being of which, up to that moment, they had been ignorant. This being so, it is not surprising that, when Jesus of Nazareth appeared, no single mind could encompass the whole of him, no single artist could paint the definitive portrait. What we have in the New Testament is a collection of fragments of memory and interpretation concerning Jesus, extruded through longstanding Jewish hermeneutical processes.[2] Early Christians, believing that in Jesus all of God's promises were fulfilled (2 Cor. 1:20), added to this tradition, searching the Hebrew scriptures for passages that could be interpreted christologically.

At quite an early period in their corporate existence, before they called themselves Christians, the fellowship of disciples of Jesus in Jerusalem followed what they called the Way—the way of faith and life initiated by Jesus (see Acts 9:2; 19:9; also 18:25). This expression was not unprecedented in Judaism; it is found, for example, in the ancient Jewish writings known as the Dead Sea Scrolls as a designation for the Qumran community's faith and life, and may be understood as a shortened version of "the true way"

---

1. Schweitzer, *Quest of the Historical Jesus*, 403.
2. For information on *testimonia*, *pesher*, typology, midrash, and other Jewish interpretive techniques, see my discussion in *Securing Life*, 176–79.

or "the right way." As companions of the Way, the followers of Jesus found themselves assessing the place of Jesus in God's unfolding purpose for humanity. With increasing clarity they saw his identity and role foreshadowed in the Jewish scriptures, especially as he had taught them how to understand those scriptures.

Jesus as Lord

At the heart of Christianity stands an affirmation that is without parallel in the monotheistic tradition: "Jesus is Lord." This statement, believed by scholars to be an early Christian creed, contains a striking confession, indicating that the first followers of Jesus viewed him as an extraordinary human, one whose influence exceeded that of human rulers (the imperial Ceasars) as the power and authority of God exceeds that of humans.

C. S. Lewis, a former atheist who converted to evangelical Christianity and gained fame as an apologist for traditional Christianity in the mid-twentieth century, famously argued that three options—and three alone—are available for people in thinking about Jesus Christ: either he was a liar, a self-deceived lunatic, or else he was what Christians have traditionally affirmed, Son of God, Lord of all, and therefore God in human flesh. Despite my appreciation for Lewis and his distinctive writings, I find these options inadequately narrow and woefully misguided, for Jesus does not literally fit any of these categories. They emerge from the perspective of the Precritical Paradigm, from reading the Gospels as if they were straightforward historical documents.

Such a reading distorts the image of Jesus, for it focuses exclusively on his deity, emphasizing the miraculous—especially the virgin birth and the physical bodily resurrection. Concentrating on the saving significance of Jesus' death (that he died for our sins), this approach concludes that Jesus and Christianity are the only way of salvation. Furthermore, it places head knowledge—belief—at the center of Christianity, stressing that to be a Christian requires affirmation that all of the above are factually true.

Modern scholarship discounts such narrow understanding of Jesus and views literalistic interpretations of scripture as misleading. In our attempts to rethink our understanding of Jesus, it is vital that we start with the humanity of Jesus (what scholars call "Christology from below")[3] rather

---

3. The term Christology refers to the Christian doctrine of the person and significance of Christ.

that with his preexistence and deity (what scholars call "Christology from above"). It is possible to move from the humanity of Jesus to his divinity, but not from his divinity to his humanity. That was the path available to the first believers, and the only path available to us. The key is to begin where the first Christians began, with their relationship with Jesus of Nazareth, the teacher and role model they knew, trusted, and loved, and then to press forward with the development of that understanding in understanding the church's experience of Christ. If we start with Jesus, we understand better who we are as humans and what we can become. If we start with Christ, we stand to lose our present and our future, our human actuality as well as our human potentiality.

As Martin Luther noted: The "humanity [of Jesus] is our holy ladder, by which we ascend to the knowledge of God. . . . Who wishes safely to ascend to the love and knowledge of God . . . let him first exercise himself in the humanity of Christ."[4] For Luther, "The scriptures begin very gently, and lead us on to Christ as a man, and then to one who is Lord over all creatures, and after that to one who is God. So do I enter delightfully, and learn to know God. But the [church] philosophers and doctors have insisted on beginning from above, and so they have become fools. We must begin from below, and after that come upwards."[5]

There are, as Luther indicates, two types of Christology, "from below" and "from above." Both types can be expressed in orthodox or in heterodox ways, and both are present in the New Testament: The earliest heretical movements in Christianity, however, tended to overspiritualize Jesus, dissociating the spiritual Christ from the physical Jesus and thereby attempting to detach Christianity from history. Such views, gnostic in nature, found agreement in docetic views of Christ, denying he was ever a true human being. A basic conviction of the Greco-Roman world was that truth, eternal and supernatural, was changeless, and that it could not (or should not) be tied to ephemeral phenomena or transitory events. By inserting the name "Pontius Pilate," the Roman procurator who authorized the crucifixion of Jesus, into the second article of the Apostles' Creed, orthodox Christians were emphasizing the historicity of the Christian faith as grounded in a series of historical events while counteracting dualistic views of reality.

---

4. Luther, *Weimarer Ausgabe* 57.99.3; cited in Hamilton, *New Essence of Christianity*, 88.

5. Luther, *Weimarer Ausgabe* 10/I 2.297.5; English translation taken from Mackintosh, *Person of Jesus Christ*, 232.

Traditional Christianity has had a large stake in historicity. From the start, much of classical Christology—particularly the doctrine of the two natures—has depended on being able to regard the words and deeds of Jesus in the Gospels as actual and reliable, and the resurrection, equated with the empty tomb as historical fact, has been seen as the hinge of the Christian faith. Yet modern Christians cannot escape the evaluation of critical biblical scholarship, which asserts that there is no certainty that Jesus did or said most of the things attributed to him in scripture.

The skepticism of the postmodern ethos, which questions traditional language about the mystery of Christ, has shattered the beliefs of the past, reducing universal religious, metaphysical, and moral truths to tentative, private, and subjective claims and opinions. The classic way of expressing ultimate reality had been to use the vocabulary of uniqueness, of finality, of timeless perfection. That Christian theology presented Jesus Christ as *the* Son of God and *the* Son of Man, *the* Alpha and *the* Omega, in whom all lines meet uniquely, perfectly, and finally. Our world, however, relativistic, pluralistic, and diverse, compels us to be more modest about our claims. For many today, to go on saying the same things in the old terms is to be in danger of rendering Christ meaningless, the answer to questions few are asking.

Thankfully, as we are discovering, the static model of reality is largely unbiblical, the imposition of a later and alien culture. The Bible is much more at home with God as active and dynamic, who confronts humans in and through the particularities and peculiarities of the here and now. The Bible does not portray God as one who is unmoved by human need, who lags behind social and biological change, but as one who is characteristically found on the shifting frontiers of such change and need, incarnated in mundane and timely events rather than in a timeless absolute beyond them all.

With regard to the historical Jesus, two closely connected questions arise: "What *can* we know of him?" and "What do we *need* to know?" The latter question, of course, is significantly more important. Our intent is not to reduce God or Christ to our level, but to relocate "the beyond" and "the ancient," the absolute and the metaphysical, to our midst. This does not mean denying the dimension of transcendence or the supernatural, but it does mean starting where modern skeptics and postmodern seekers might have the best chance of encounter. It means beginning with the familiar and the contingent. In this process, the claims of honesty and integrity, of justice and freedom, of solidarity with universal suffering may be taken seriously and without reserve. One may not see how it all adds up or discern any final truths or laws that cannot be broken, but in the particular, concrete situation, one knows that persons matter more than procedures, principles more than precepts.

Today, in our cultural milieu, the place of theology in general and of Christology and soteriology in particular, is the servants' quarters, not, as in the period of Christendom, the throne. Its style will be more modest, more broken. Yet at its center is a figure, as the author of Hebrews insists he always is, who is "suited to our need" (Heb. 7:26, NEB), and whom in all his humiliation Christians still rightly call "Teacher" and "Master" (John 13:13).

Whatever more he is—or was—he must be one of us. If Jesus is to be our Person, our Man, he must be a human being in every sense of the word. This is what we find in the New Testament. The early Christians began with a view of Christ that was uncomplicated and relatable. They certainly did not see Jesus to be of *merely* human significance, since he embodied what God was doing in their midst. But their earliest memory was fashioned into a simplistic Christology, perhaps the earliest, of "a man," Jesus of Nazareth, singled out by God, crucified and raised from the dead, as Peter's speech on the day of Pentecost recalls (Acts 2:22–24). "This Jesus God raised up, and of that all of us are witnesses. Being therefore exalted at the right hand of God, and having received from the Father the promise of the Holy Spirit, he has poured out this that you both see and hear" (Acts 2:32–33).

John Knox has made the point that as long as this primitive "adoptionist" or "exaltationist" Christology prevailed, "the simple actuality of the humanity was in no sense or degree compromised. Not only could it be whole and intact, but it was also subject to no theological or mythological pressure of any kind."[6] But the pressure began soon thereafter, when the idea that the death of Jesus was according to "the definite plan and foreknowledge of God" (Acts 2:23) became translated as the preexistence of Christ. As soon as Jesus Christ was, or could be, represented as a preexistent being who had come down from heaven, then the genuineness of his humanity while he was on earth was open to question. Not that his followers actually questioned his humanity, for the memory was too strong. From the beginning of theological reflection on the significance of Jesus there was the insistence on his solidarity with humanity; otherwise his relevance for

---

6. Knox, *Humanity and Divinity of Christ*, 6–7.

us would be undercut. Nevertheless, the threat to his humanity was there, precisely because of the story told about him to bring out the significance of his humanity for our salvation.

Who, then, was Jesus, and what, from the historical records, can we infer about him? Despite belonging to the Jewish peasant class, he was minimally literate, in that he undoubtedly went to school in the synagogue in Nazareth, where the emphasis would have been on reading and writing, with the Torah as the primary text. He became a woodworker, which, in terms of social standing, placed him at the lower end of the peasant class, more marginalized than a peasant who still owned a small piece of land.

At some point in his life Jesus embarked upon a religious quest. He probably underwent what William James calls a "conversion experience," not, of course, from paganism to Judaism, for he grew up Jewish. Conversion, as James defines it, need not infer a change from one religion to another, or from being nonreligious to being religious. It can refer to a process of internal transformation, whether sudden or gradual, which led him to undertake his ministry. Influenced by a fiery preacher known as John the Baptist, in his late twenties or around the age of thirty he embarked on his career. Mark dates the beginning of Jesus' ministry to John's arrest, which suggests that, with his mentor in prison, Jesus stepped in to carry on.

What was the adult Jesus like, and what did he come to understand about himself and his mission? All understandings of Christianity rely ultimately on two assessments: Jesus' self-understanding and the early church's conceptualizing of that self-understanding. Let us start with the obvious: Jesus was deeply Jewish. Not only was he Jewish by birth and socialization, but he remained a Jew all of his life. His scripture was the Jewish Bible. He did not intend to establish a new religion, but saw himself as having a mission within Judaism. He spoke as a Jew to other Jews. His early followers were Jewish.

Jesus became a gifted teacher. His verbal gifts were remarkable. His language was most often metaphorical, poetic, and imaginative, filled with memorable short sayings and compelling short stories we call parables. He was clearly exceptionally intelligent. Like the classical prophets of ancient Israel, he performed symbolic actions: on one occasion he staged a demonstration in the temple, overturning the tables of the money changers and driving out the sellers of sacrificial animals. There was a radical social and political edge to his message and activity, as he challenged the social order of his day and indicted the elites who dominated it. He must have been remarkably courageous, willing to continue what he was doing even when in lethal danger. He was a remarkable healer: more healing stories are told about him than about anybody else in the Jewish tradition. He attracted a following, which means he was quite compelling. He also attracted enemies, especially among the rich and powerful. Unlike the founders of the world's other major religious traditions, his public ministry was brief, lasting at most three or four years. Living only into his early thirties, he was then crucified on charges of sedition. At his crucifixion the Romans placed an inscription on his cross that read, "Jesus of Nazareth, King of the Jews," thereby issuing a warning to his followers that Roman rule would not tolerate insurrection.

Though it is hard to believe, some Christians are unaware of the Jewishness of Jesus, or, if they are aware, either downplay it or obscure that reality with later Christian anti-Semitism. The separation of Jesus from Judaism has had tragic consequences for Jews throughout the centuries, and any faithful image of Jesus must take with utmost seriousness his rootedness in Judaism. If we fail to understand Jesus as a Jewish figure teaching and acting within Judaism, we will misunderstand his mission.

As a result of reading the New Testament, filtered through the creeds of later Christendom, Christians have arrived at an understanding of Jesus that is quite different from the sketch presented above. That understanding might be summarized under the phrase "Christian messiah," an exalted status that includes such titles of Jesus as "Son of God," "Word of God," "Wisdom of God," "Lamb of God," "Light of the World," "Bread of Life," "Alpha and Omega," and "firstborn of all creation." These may not convey what Jesus of Nazareth thought or taught about himself, but they came to summarize what New Testament Christians believed Jesus to be.

The Gospels, as the rest of the New Testament, are products of developing traditions of the early Christian communities in which they were written. As such, they contain two types of information: *history remembered*, meaning some of the things reported in the Gospels really happened and reliably represent Jesus as a figure of history, and *history metaphorized*, meaning some of the tradition is not literally true but represents the revised understanding of the communities themselves following Easter. Biblical scholarship distinguishes between these two understandings of Jesus by speaking of "the Jesus of history" and "the Christ of faith." Marcus Borg, in his writings, substitutes the phrase "the pre-Easter Jesus" for the historical Jesus and "post-Easter Jesus" for the "Jesus" of Christian tradition and experience. The latter includes both "the canonical Jesus" we meet on the surface level of the New Testament and "the creedal Jesus" we encounter in the classic Christian creeds of the fourth and fifth centuries. For Borg both pre- and post-Easter understandings of Jesus are valid, the first as the community's memory of the historical Jesus and the second as the community's testimony of Jesus. In other words, after his death, Jesus the Galilean Jew became in the experience and language of his followers "the face of God" and ultimately the second person of the Trinity.

This conceptual transformation may be viewed as a three-fold process; early Christian thinking about Jesus began with (1) experience, and then moved through (2) metaphorical expression to (3) conceptual formulation. In the beginning was experience, that of the disciples and others of Jesus. The primary cause of the transition from the pre-Easter to the post-Easter Jesus was the Easter experience, expressed by the early Christian conviction that "God raised Jesus from the dead." Though the gospel stories portray this as occurring literally, "the core meaning of Easter is that Jesus continued to be experienced after his death, but in a radically new way: as a spiritual and divine reality."[7]

The Easter experience led to a transformed perception of Jesus among his followers. In the sixty or seventy years after Jesus' death, when the traditions found in the New Testament took shape, Jewish Christian communities searched the Hebrew scriptures, finding a large number of metaphors or images that related to Jesus and his significance, images such as servant of God, lamb of God, light of the world, bread of life, Lord, door, vine, shepherd, messiah, savior, great high priest, sacrifice, Son of God, Son of Man, Wisdom of God, and Word of God. Over time, these metaphors became the subject of intellectual reflection and conceptualization. Some, ultimately, became doctrine. This process produced the post-Easter Jesus—the "Christ of faith"—of Christian tradition.

Jewish Images of Jesus

As a first-century Palestinian Jew, Jesus belonged to a world where religion (theology) and politics went hand in hand. The theology was Jewish monotheism, a doctrine forged through centuries of subjugation and persecution, going back to the Babylonian exile. First-century Jews held their monotheism passionately. Theirs was not an abstract theory about the

---

7. Borg, *God We Never Knew*, 93.

existence of one God. They believed their God, Yahweh, was the only God, and that all others were idols. A corollary of monotheism was "election," the belief that the Jews had been chosen by this one God, making what happened to Israel of universal significance. Many Jews of Jesus' day believed that God was about to vindicate them, understanding this act as having global implications, as the means of divine judgment and/or mercy upon the rest of the world.

Monotheists, who believe in one God and in their status as God's elect people, while currently suffering oppression, would also believe the present state of affairs temporary. Monotheism and election thus give birth to eschatology, a perspective that views history as purposeful and therefore as moving toward a climactic resolution or restoration, at which time everything would be made right. First-century Jewish eschatology claimed that Yahweh would soon act within history to vindicate his people and to establish permanent justice and peace. This belief included the great promises of forgiveness articulated by biblical prophets, notably Isaiah, Jeremiah, and Ezekiel. The so-called post-exilic writings spoke of a restoration still to be described, a liberation they described as a new exodus.

In keeping with this understanding, it follows that Jesus of Nazareth might have viewed his mission as prophetic, announcing, like John the Baptist before him, God's coming kingdom. But Jesus, it seems, went beyond John's verbal role, embodying in his person and his ministry the presence of that kingdom. For Jesus, the all-encompassing rule of God was near, which when it came in its fullness, would restore Israel's role as "light to the nations" and challenge evil in all its manifestations, political, social, and economic. The coming kingdom of God was not a new sort of religion, a new moral code, or a new soteriology (a doctrine about how one might go to heaven after death). Nor was it a new sociological analysis, critique, or agenda. It was about Israel's story reaching its climax, about Israel's history moving toward its decisive moment.[8]

E. P. Sanders, in his classic text *Jesus and Judaism*, maintains that before the outbreak of the War of the Jews against Rome in AD 66, "common Judaism" held the following hopes for the future: the restoration of the tribes of Israel; the conversion, destruction, or subjugation of the Gentiles; the renewal of Jerusalem, including a new or rebuilt temple; and the purification of God's people and their worship.[9] Whatever one makes of

---

8. Borg and Wright, *Meaning of Jesus*, 31–35.
9. Sanders, *Jesus and Judaism*, 279–303.

his idea of a common Judaism, surely the beliefs Sanders highlights were widespread among Jesus' contemporaries, as was apocalyptic eschatology in general. According to Sanders, Jesus was an apocalyptic prophet standing in the tradition of Jewish restoration theology. He shared the beliefs common in Judaism, together with this prevailing understanding of Israel's story and hope. Having established the essential Jewishness of Jesus on this topic, Sanders finds primitive Christianity to be a movement in continuity with Jesus' hopes and expectations: "The most certain fact of all is that early Christianity was an eschatological movement."[10]

Marcus Borg represents a growing number of modern scholars who challenge this understanding of Jesus, envisioning instead a non-eschatological Jesus, whose role, if interpreted prophetically, should be limited to that of a social prophet engaged in radical social criticism. According to this model, Jesus was a counter-cultural revolutionary who opposed the domination systems of his day both in person and through an alternative community of disciples, chosen to represent the New Israel of God. In Borg's view the kingdom of God represents a this-worldly social vision—a vision that empowers Christians and defines the church's ongoing role in society—rather than an other-worldly eschatological vision imposed from above and occasioned by a church raptured from this earth, an interpretation popular in many American fundamentalist and evangelical circles today.

Viewing Jesus as a deeply Jewish but non-eschatological figure, Borg challenges another vital element in the popular image of Jesus, namely that Jesus understood himself to be the messiah. According to Borg, the pre-Easter Jesus consistently pointed away from himself to God; his message was theocentric, not christocentric, meaning that he was centered in God and not in messianic pronouncements about himself. On the basis of these two denials of popular but what he considers erroneous images of Jesus, Borg suggests five models in the Jewish tradition that accurately portray the self-understanding of the historical (pre-Easter) Jesus:[11]

1. Jesus as *mystic*: Like Moses, Elijah, and the prophets, Jesus was a "Spirit person," a "mediator of the sacred." This notion, which he calls the most crucial fact about Jesus, means that Jesus was one of those

---

10. Sanders, "Jesus: His Religious Type," 6.

11. Borg, *God We Never Knew*, 89–90. A fuller discussion is found in Borg and Wright, *Meaning of Jesus*, 60–76.

persons in human history to whom the sacred was, to use William James's terms, firsthand religious experience rather than a second-hand belief.

2. Jesus as *healer and exorcist*: The evidence that Jesus performed paranormal healings is very strong; in fact, more healing stories are told about him than about any other figure in the Jewish tradition. While admitting that psychosomatic factors may sometimes have been involved, Borg avoids usage of the term "miracle" in connection with Jesus, since the latter requires accepting a supernatural interventionist model of God. "Interventions, no. Marvels, yes."[12]

3. Jesus as *wisdom teacher*: Using provocative saying and memorable parables, Jesus taught a subversive and alternative wisdom. Conventional Jewish wisdom was based upon the dynamics of retribution, that is, rewards and punishments. Unlike conventional wisdom teachers, who pass on and sometimes elaborate the received traditions or conventions of a community or group, Jesus invited hearers into a different way of seeing—God, themselves, and life itself. His wisdom teaching invited people to live in the Spirit, to walk a path of transformation centered in the Spirit.

4. Jesus as *social prophet*: Like the social prophets of the Hebrew Bible (Amos, Micah, Jeremiah), Jesus criticized the economic, political, and religious elites of his time. Advocating an alternative social vision grounded in the compassion of God, he was often in conflict with authorities. In speaking of the kingdom of God, he used a political metaphor that contrasted existing kingdoms: the kingdom of God is what life would be like on earth if God were king, rather than Herod and Caesar.

5. Jesus as *movement founder*: Jesus brought into being a Jewish renewal or revitalization movement that challenged and shattered the social boundaries of his day, a movement that eventually became the early Christian church. Although his public activity was very brief, Jesus formed an embryonic group whose inclusiveness and egalitarian practice embodied his alternative social vision.

It is not pedagogically acceptable to commingle eschatological and noneschatological perspectives of Jesus. Either his mindset was

12. Borg and Wright, *Meaning of Jesus*, 67.

eschatological or it was not, and for that reason modern scholarship does not allow fence-sitting on the matter. There is no question in my mind that Jesus was clearly driven by current Jewish eschatological expectations and that he organized his ministry around those conceptions. As an eschatological prophet, however, he brought the entire package of prophecy to bear on his task, meaning that through his work and ministry he believed he was inaugurating and embodying the works of the kingdom. The kingdom need not be seen as a strictly "end-time" phenomenon, however, for in a spiritual sense the kingdom is found in whole nowhere, but in part everywhere.

While the kingdom was embryonically present in Jesus, it cannot be said to have been fully present in him. As Jesus made clear in his parables, the kingdom is an expanding (unfolding) phenomenon. Like yeast in dough, the kingdom must grow continuously until all is leavened (Matt. 13:33; Luke 13:21). Every age must announce its coming and commit fully to its hopeful vision. In every age, all who seek the kingdom are its citizens and every messenger is holy. Whether we depict Jesus eschatologically, noneschatologically, or as the culmination of both mindsets, in every respect Jesus was a Jewish figure of his day.

The Human Bridge to God

As noted in my earlier publication on biblical Christology,[13] there is no more important topic for inquiry today than the meaning and message of Jesus, no more important concern than one's answer to Jesus' perennial question, "Who do you say that I am?" (Mark 8:29), for in this quest, I believe, lies the solution to individual malaise and humanity's woes.

If, as some theologians suggest, humans cannot know God directly, how then can we know God? The biblical answer is through Jesus, for he is the bridge that connects the profane and the sacred, the human with the divine. If humans wish to grasp the character and will of God, the New Testament writers affirm, they need only look to Jesus, "the pioneer and perfecter of our faith" (Heb. 12:2), for Jesus is the best picture ever taken of God. The fundamental affirmation of Christianity is that Jesus is the clue to the mystery of Christ, just as Christ is the clue to the mystery of God and the meaning of human existence. For those who call themselves Christians, the human Jesus is decisive for interpreting Christ, just as Christ is decisive for understanding God.

13. Vande Kappelle, *Scandal of Divine Love*.

One of the central teachings of Christian anthropology is that humans are made in the "image of God." In the first chapter of Genesis we read these words: "Let us make humankind in our image, according to our likeness; and let them have dominion over . . . the earth" (Gen. 1:26). While it is not clear what it means to say that humans are made in the "image" of God—that idea is never systematically explained in the Bible—it cannot refer to physical likeness, for the writer of Genesis 1 takes pains to stress the holiness and transcendence of God. Nevertheless, that concept clearly is central to what it means to be human. Concerning the phrase "image of God" (often referred to by the Latin phrase *Imago Dei*), the following meanings have been suggested:

- Humankind's nature: Because humans are created in the image of God, they have a moral and spiritual nature. Having a God-given freedom provides both dignity and responsibility.

- Humankind's position: Being made in the image of God implies personhood and attributes to human beings a unique relationship with God. As persons, humans are related to God in a manner different from anything else in the created order.

- Humankind's function: Since human beings are uniquely related to God by creation, the Old Testament states that their primary function is to worship and serve the Creator in every aspect of life. Furthermore, as God's vice-regents, they are given ecological responsibility over nature.

- The universality of the image: Genesis 1:27 tells us that both male and female are created in God's image. In the creation account, Adam and Eve represent all humanity. Indeed, the word "Adam" is not a proper name in Hebrew, but merely a word meaning "humankind." Likewise, the word "Eve" is the Hebrew word for "life" or "living." The *Imago Dei* is not the sole possession of one tribe or race or nation. Its potential applies to every human being without exception.

According to this understanding, while we humans are *in* nature, we stand *above* nature, for we have the freedom to acknowledge the claims of the Creator upon us and, within that relationship, to exercise dominion over the earth. Because they stand in a personal relation with God, humans are the crowning glory of God's creation (Ps. 8:5–8).

How then does Jesus fit into this perspective? Who is Jesus Christ, and why is he so important for the Christian faith? The Christian doctrine known as Christology sets out to explore why the church believes that Jesus of Nazareth, a first-century Galilean peasant, holds the key to the nature of God and of human destiny. Christology is not simply about Jesus, though even as human he represents the ideal universal person, the embodiment of the highest and best in us all. Christology is also about Christ, in whom "all things hold together" (Col. 1:17). Such understanding has very much to do with us today. If Christology is to be relevant today, it must relate to the central issues of our day, providing vision, focus, and coherence not only to religious concerns but also to political, economic, social, scientific, and aesthetic concerns as well. If we are interested in Christology, it should be because of the vital issues of our day, not despite them. If, as psychiatrist Carl Jung, puts it, the Christ-figure corresponds to the archetype of the self, the God-image in us all, then this universality of the Christ figure, representing the ultimate dimensions of human existence, alone makes Christology relevant today. In this sense, the discussion about Jesus addresses the relationship between the self and God, the mystery that lies at the center of reality. At this initial point in the discussion, the mystery of the Christ is not a matter of faith but rather one of recognition, not "Can you believe this individual to be the Son of God?" (that question comes later), but "Can you see the fullness of your humanity in him?"

The first Christians had a stunning array of titles, names, and expressions for Jesus, ranging from Rabbi, Messiah, and High Priest to Lord, Son of God, Word of God, Wisdom of God, and Spirit of God. In addition to established titles, most books of the New Testament introduce unique titles of their own. In the Pauline corpus alone we find a broad range of christological titles. In 1 Corinthians, for example, in addition to common titles such as God, Lord, Messiah, and Spirit we find also Head (12:12–13), Rock (10:4), Destroyer (10:10); Man of Heaven (15:49); Power of God (1:18); and Wisdom of God (1:21). In 2 Corinthians we find also Glory (4:4) and Image of God (4:4), and that's only a start to the Pauline list. Colossians speaks of Christ as Firstborn (1:15); Beginning (1:18); and Fullness of God (1:19).

Over the next three centuries these titles would be fleshed out to incorporate a Nicene understanding: Jesus Christ was of the same substance as God the Father; he was equal with God in status, authority, and power; he was the one through whom God created all things in heaven and on earth; there never was a time when he did not exist. These were all quite exalted things to say about an apocalyptic itinerant preacher from rural Galilee crucified as a would-be messiah, a failed claimant to the vacant Jewish throne of Judea.

By AD 381, this understanding of Jesus, recited in the Nicene Creed, served as a benchmark of orthodoxy for all succeeding mainstream Christian churches, whether Catholic, Orthodox, or Protestant. The classic Christian position, summarized in the "doctrine of the two natures," perfectly divine and perfectly human, was definitively stated by the Council of Chalcedon in 451. Generally stated, this position affirms the centrality of the two natures of Jesus Christ for the church, wisely noting that so long as we recognize that Jesus Christ is both truly divine and truly human, the precise manner in which this is articulated or explored is not of fundamental importance. Chalcedon defined the starting point for classical Christology to be the recognition that in the face of Christ we find the face of God.

As stunning as these claims remain, what is even more surprising is the rapidness of the development of the early church's Christology. According to biblical scholar Martin Hengel, more happened in the first decade or two after the death of Jesus than in the entire later centuries-long development of dogma. The historian of early Christianity, Bart Ehrman, concurs: "It must have been no more than twenty years after Jesus died, possibly even fewer, that the Christ poem in Philippians [2:6–11] was composed, in which Jesus was said to have been a preexistent being 'in the form of God' who became human and then because of his obedient death was exalted to divine status and made equal with God, the Lord to whom all people on earth would bow in worship and confess loyalty."[14]

During subsequent centuries, Christian thinkers devoted a great deal of study to the topic of Christology, speculating about the two natures of Christ while closely connecting their study to doctrines of the incarnation, the atonement, and the Trinity. Over time, two main pictures developed: of a Christ who was God in disguise and of Jesus the perfect man. Sadly, both pictures, offered as objects of devotion and belief, distanced Jesus from ordinary people and led to his irrelevance for increasing numbers of people.

Dietrich Bonhoeffer spoke for many when he wrote from a Nazi prison in the 1940s: "What really bothers me incessantly is the question . . . who Christ really is for us today." For Jesus Christ to be "the same yesterday and today and forever" (Heb. 13:8), he has to be a contemporary of every

---

14. Ehrman, *How Jesus Became God*, 370.

generation and therefore different for every generation: he must be *their* Christ, *our* Christ.

The critical question is, "How does the 'Christ for us today' relate to the Christ for other ages—whether of the first century or the sixteenth or the twentieth?" One mistake of the liberal tradition is to wish too fervently that the biblical writers might say exactly what needs to be said today. It is the same error in reverse of the traditionalists who wish too fervently that the biblical message might be the exact word we ought to pronounce now. Our exploration of the meaning of Jesus Christ—then and now—presupposes a reality there to explore. According to a Quaker observation, "we do not 'seek' the Atlantic, we explore it." The same applies to Christ. Christians begin with a given, gracious reality. They cannot assume this dogmatically or narrowly, nor can they presuppose it of others. When Paul and other early Christians state, often uncritically, "to me, living is Christ" (Phil. 1:21), or confess, "Jesus is Lord" (1 Cor. 12:3), what did these mean to first-century Christians, and what do they mean to us today? The center, thankfully, is given in scripture, but the periphery is teasingly and liberatingly open.

In the words of J. M. Creed: "Christian theology need not claim that the Christian religion contains within itself all truth, or even all truth that is of religious value, but if it loses the conviction that in Jesus Christ it has found the deepest truth of God, it has lost itself."[15]

The Triple Office (*munus triplex*) of Jesus

Throughout church history, Christians have found in the Old Testament a basis for recognizing in Jesus the *munus triplex* (triple office) of anointed prophet, priest, and king. Present in the writings of patristic and medieval theologians, this theme of Christ's "triple office" was developed by John Calvin (1509–1564) and articulated by other Protestant and Roman Catholic thinkers, including Cardinal John Henry Newman (1801–1890) and the documents of the Second Vatican Council (1962–1965).

The important element in the ministry of Jesus is that he not only lived according to the highest standards, but he inspired others to follow his example. If the christological quest offers a window not only into the person and work of Jesus but also into the fullness of our own human potential, the triple office represents a starting-point, for like Jesus, we too are called to ministries that are prophetic, priestly, and royal in nature. Like the

---

15. Creed, *Divinity of Jesus Christ*, 113.

prophets of old, Jesus calls his followers to speak forth boldly and without compromise against disobedience and disbelief within the social, religious, and political establishment. Like priests, Jesus calls his followers to live sacrificially, advocating for the needs of the disadvantaged and marginalized in society. Like citizens of God's kingdom on earth, Jesus calls his followers to announce the uncompromising standards of God's love and justice, embodying the ideals of that kingdom in our own values, priorities, and lifestyles, reminding our fellow humans in word and deed to be loyal to the royal within, for to be human is to be made in the image of God. No matter one's race, creed, sexual persuasion, or status in life, all humans are children of God and therefore kin in God's kindom.

Going Deeper: Reflection for Participants

1. Assess your understanding of the author's statement that "The whole of the New Testament—every book, chapter, and verse—is theology."

2. Do you agree with Albert Schweitzer's statement that Jesus can only be known by faith? Support your answer.

3. The author argues that many Christians fail to grasp the "Jewishness of Jesus." In your estimation, what does he mean by that expression?

4. Are the Gospels reliable eyewitness accounts? Support your answer.

5. Many Christians find C. S. Lewis's three options concerning Jesus persuading; the author finds them to be misguided. Upon reading the chapter, do you side with Lewis or with the author on this matter? Support your answer.

6. The Gospels are said to contain two types of information: history remembered and history metaphorized. Explain the differences between them and assess their value.

7. E. P. Sanders viewed Jesus to be an eschatological prophet, whereas Marcus Borg envisioned a non-eschatological Jesus. Assuming you cannot sit on a fence on this issue, with whom do you agree? Explain your answer.

8. If you had to choose one, which of Borg's models of Jesus do you find most compelling as an explanation of Jesus' historical ministry? Support your answer.

9. What does this chapter say about humans as bearers of the image of God?

10. How do Jesus' life and ministry inform your life and ministry?

11. If Jesus were to appear in our midst today, what would he want us to know about his nature and his mission?

12. In your estimation, what is the primary insight gained from this session?

Session 6

Rethinking Scripture
Revelation or Revolution?

Getting Started

Homework Assignment: Answer the following question, writing your answer in your journal. Be prepared to share your views with others in the class. 1. Is the Bible divinely inspired, humanly inspired, or somehow jointly inspired? Support your answer.

Gaining Momentum

Christians have always affirmed a close relationship between the Bible and God, just as other religions affirm a close connection between the sacred and their holy scriptures. Foundational to reading the Bible is a decision about how to view its origin. Is it a divine product, a human product, or somehow both?

    Building on the conviction that divine revelation and man-made religion are fundamentally irreconcilable, many Christians believe that the only choice a person can make about the Bible is to view it either as the infallible, inerrant word of God or as a collection of fairy tales with little or no value for modern people. Since the latter is what unbelievers think, fundamentalist Christians believe they must view the Bible as God's very word of truth, defending it in all respects, even on historical and scientific matters. For many, the Bible's reliability is so critical that they will argue, "If I can't believe the Bible when it speaks about creation or history, then how can I believe it about Jesus Christ and salvation?" To frame the question of the inspiration and authority of the Bible in this manner, however, is to do an injustice to the traditional doctrines of the inspiration and authority of scripture.

Acknowledging the obvious human element in the Bible, modern Christians generally take a both/and stance regarding biblical authorship: The Bible is both divine and human. However, this approach is also problematic. Viewing the Bible as both divine and human leaves us two options. One option is to say that it is all divine and all human. That may sound good, but no one maintains such an unworkable tension. The other, more typical option is to attempt to separate the divine parts from the human parts—as if some come from God and others are human. The parts that come from God are then given greater authority. However, who is to say which parts are divine and which human? The Bible does not come with footnotes that say, "This passage reflects the will of God; the next passage does not." Therefore, those who take the entire Bible as divine are consistent, but they might be consistently wrong.

How, for instance, does one understand the Ten Commandments? Most Christians who think of the Bible as both divine and human would say that the commandments come from God. Does that mean that they are equally authoritative? If so, all Christians should worship God on Saturday, since that is the day clearly in mind as the day of worship. There is biblical evidence that the sanctity of the Sabbath was in effect among the Israelites prior to the revelation of the commandments to Moses on Mount Sinai (cf. Exod. 16:22–30). And if the Ten Commandments are divinely inspired, why are they written from a male point of view (for instance, they prohibit coveting your neighbor's wife but say nothing about coveting your neighbor's husband)? Furthermore, the commandments against stealing, adultery, murder, bearing false witness, and so forth are simply rules that make it possible for humans to live together in community. Biblical scholarship affirms that the pattern upon which these commandments are based is a treaty pattern devised by the Hittites, a powerful empire that predated Moses and came to an end prior to the time of Moses. Divine genius is not required to come up with rules like these. This is not to say that the Ten Commandments are unimportant, but rather that their origin is human.[1]

---

1. Borg, *Reading the Bible*, 26–27.

Modern scholars view the Bible as the product of two faith communities, each responding uniquely to divine revelation. The Bible, therefore, contains ancient Israel's perceptions and misperceptions, just as it contains the early Christian movement's perceptions and misperceptions. Likewise, the Gospels, which record the account of Jesus, reflect not static truths but rather changing theological perspectives. Moreover, these texts are not the words of eyewitnesses, as is often claimed, but were shaped by the events of the second half of the first century, perhaps even more dramatically than by the events of the time in which Jesus actually lived.

Biblical Inspiration

When traditional Christians call the Bible the Word of God,[2] they generally assume its inspiration. The point of inspiration is that it gives the biblical text the same authority as if the words came from the mouth of God. If scripture were no longer considered inspired, it would cease being God's Word for them. If the Bible were not God's Word, students, scholars, and progressive thinkers might study it as inspiring literature but, having lost its mystique, it would be abandoned by "Bible-reading" Christians.

As important as biblical inspiration is to most Christians, when pressed to define the concept, some might reply with a shrug of the shoulders, others with a vague reference to the divine origin of the Bible, and still others might allude to 2 Timothy 3:16–17: "All scripture is inspired by God and is useful for teaching, for reproof, for correction, and for training in righteousness, so that everyone who belongs to God may be proficient, equipped for every good work." Conservative scholars note that the Greek word translated as "inspired" here literally means "God-breathed," a reference traditionally taken to mean that the authors were directed by God to produce documents that accurately reflected God's message to humanity. While many understand the term inspiration to describe something that happened to the authors, literalists note that this verse bypasses the authors and their humanity, speaking only of the written product as inspired.

---

2. Keep in mind that none of the authors of the books in the Bible wrote thinking they were writing the "Word of God." That was something decided much later. Furthermore, there is only one reference to "Word of God" in the Bible as a whole, and that reference does not concern written scripture but rather Jesus of Nazareth, as we find in the opening verses of the Gospel of John (John 1:1, 14; see Rev. 19:13). For Christians traditionally, the canonical Bible is a witness that points to the Word. In so doing, it points away from itself.

Another passage Christians often cite is 2 Peter 1:20–21: "First of all you must understand this, that no prophecy of scripture is a matter of one's own interpretation, because no prophecy ever came by human will, but men and women moved by the Holy Spirit spoke from God." Verse 21 describes the inspiration process as one in which the human authors were "moved" by the Holy Spirit. In biblical times, the Greek verb used here referred to the moving of a ship's sails by the wind, an apt biblical metaphor for the role of the Holy Spirit.

The implications of such an inspired Bible for theology are enormous: God exists, God is benevolent, and God communicates directly with us, endowing us with providential resources and values to safeguard our dignity and identity. Such inspiration implies biblical reliability, down to tiniest details. Of course, when Christians quote scripture to authenticate its own inspiration, they practice circular reasoning, always questionable.

Theories of Inspiration

Christians who look to the Bible as a source of religious teaching or for guidance concerning how to live, bring to their reading presuppositions that affect interpretation. These presuppositions influence their understanding of inspiration and the authority of the Bible. Some church traditions say that God is the author of the Bible in the sense that God actually dictated the words of the Bible to human writers who recorded the words verbatim. This approach is called a *literalist view* of inspiration. Other church traditions hold that the human authors of the Bible are real authors in every sense, but that the words of scripture are still somehow what God wanted to communicate to humanity. This approach, called a *contextualist view* of inspiration, allows that God is the author of the Bible without specifying how the Bible is inspired, except to emphasize that the freedom, individuality, and creativity of the human authors are preserved. Of course, actual understandings of inspiration are often subtler and more complex than these approaches might suggest.

This session takes as its starting point an understanding of inspiration that accepts the full and free involvement of the Bible's human authors. This approach is called contextualist because it emphasizes that to understand scripture readers need to take into account the historical, political, cultural, literary, and religious contexts in which the documents were written. This approach is compatible with contemporary historical and literary methods of studying the Bible.

Concerning the authority of the Bible, communities and individuals that hold a contextualist approach to inspiration might say that the Bible is best described as compelling and persuasive. This means that the Bible has authority insofar as it compels us to respond with faith, hope, and love. Further, it does not legislate a particular moral action in response to specific situations, but it provides a series of guidelines upon which Christians can reflect on modern issues and concerns. William Countryman, a theologian and professor of the New Testament, explains the authority of scripture in this way: While the church participated in creating the Bible and acts as its interpreter, the Bible functions as the church's judge, constantly calling it to conversion.[3] Therefore, the authority of the Bible is closely connected to its power to transform.

Biblical scholars suggest three broad possibilities regarding the inspiration of the Bible, to which we add a fourth as corollary:

- *Verbal inspiration* – the view that every word of the Bible is divinely inspired and therefore inerrant.

- *Human response to inspiration* – the view that biblical writers were witnesses to divine revelation; their words and experiences may be human but they serve as vehicles to a higher voice and a deeper reality.

- *Inspired imagination* – the view that the Bible is great literature, designed to capture the imagination; though the books of the Bible contain heightened insight, their message is conditioned by historical, sociological, and cultural factors. When the Bible is studied academically, it is this view that scholars espouse.

Corollary:

- *Inspired process* – the view that scripture requires ongoing interpretation. This assertion, flowing naturally from the preceding options, recognizes that the sacredness of scripture is validated by its ability to inspire Christians in every age. Scripture, defined and finalized by the canonical process, has an open-ended quality both dynamic and alive, thereby extending the revelatory process to the present. Viewing scripture as "inspired process" safeguards the original revelation while authenticating its ongoing meaning.

3. Countryman, *Biblical Authority or Biblical Tyranny?*, 52–57.

The earliest Christians had no Bibles to study or read individually. It was the church, and more specifically the religious leaders of that community, that interpreted the scriptures. This was so not only because it had been the church and its leaders that had defined which texts were "scriptural," but also because the texts themselves were not intended as much for private reading as for their suitability for liturgical use. If a document was not considered revelatory, it was not to be read in church. Since most Christians were illiterate and copies of the scriptures were rare, the majority of the faithful could only hear scripture read to them in church, almost always as part of the ritual celebration of the Eucharist. It was principally through the mediation of the clergy and in the restricted context of worship that early Christians could approach scripture.

From the earliest days, Christian leaders formulated theories of biblical interpretation. By the fourth century, clearly defined interpretive theories were already widely accepted by Christian leaders, including that scripture contained four levels of meaning: literal (historical and literal level), allegorical (hidden mystical and spiritual truths), tropological (moral lessons), and anagogical (eschatological level, revealing secrets concerning the afterlife and Christ's future kingdom). While allegorical and other levels of interpretation provided Christian theology with flexibility, giving it the capacity to intertwine written and oral traditions and the ability to adapt to ever-changing situations, in the wrong hands it could be abused, leading to heterodox beliefs and practices. From the fifth through sixteenth centuries, scripture remained firmly in the hands of the church elites who had mastered the accepted exegetical methods. Major controversies were addressed by bishops through synods or councils.

The Protestant Reformers of the sixteenth century declared that the church had become corrupt because it had buried the truths of scripture beneath layers of humanly devised traditions. Claiming to base their reforms on scripture, the Reformers encouraged the translation of scripture into the vernacular, a process aided by the invention of the printing press. Martin Luther (1485–1546), a first-generation Reformer, believed that faith and the Holy Spirit's illumination were prerequisites for an interpreter of the Bible. He laid down the foundational premise of the Reformation, the principle of *sola scriptura* (scripture alone), the primacy of scripture above all other authorities. Asserting that the Bible should be viewed differently from other literature, he downplayed dependence on church authorities to understand the Bible. Luther also challenged the prevailing "rule of faith," maintaining that rather than the church determining what the scriptures teach, scripture should determine what the church teaches. He also believed that the Bible is a clear book (the "perspicuity" of scripture), in opposition to medieval dogma that the scriptures are so obscure that only the church can uncover their true meaning. He favored a literal understanding of the text, rather than the allegorical method of interpreting scripture, stressing that the interpreter should consider historical conditions, grammar, and context in the process of exegesis.

Probably the greatest exegete of the Reformation was John Calvin (1509–1564), a second-generation Reformer. Agreeing in general with the principles articulated by Luther, he too believed that spiritual illumination is necessary and regarded allegorical interpretation as a deceptive device that distorted the clear sense of scripture. Assuming the divine authorship of scripture, he adhered strictly to the principle of harmony, meaning that scripture is its own best interpreter. No passage of scripture should be set up against another; secondary and obscure passages in scripture should always be subject to primary and plain passages. He placed importance on studying the context, grammar, words, and parallel passages, stating that the primary task of an interpreter is to allow the author to speak, rather than to import one's own meaning into the text.

Espousing the priesthood of all believers, the Reformers believed every Christian capable of reading scripture, as guided individually by the Holy Spirit. Rather than leading to unanimity, however, that impetus resulted in further disagreement and fragmentation. Despite their emphasis on scripture as sole authority, the Reformers could not agree with one another on the application of scripture to polity, social issues, and sacramental practices such as baptism or the Eucharist. The unraveling of Christian unity in the sixteenth century led to the emergence of rival communities, each claiming to be the "true" church and to have the correct understanding of scripture.

The Renaissance and the Enlightenment gave rise to ideologies such as humanism, rationalism, skepticism, scientism, and existentialism, each to varying degrees undermining the authority of scripture while simultaneously unleashing a monumental critical effort to ascertain truth in scripture. Searching for truth in scripture, biblical scholars increasingly detected the humanity of the authors who wrote the documents that together constituted the Bible. As Johann Gottfried von Herder argued in the late eighteenth century, the Bible was religious literature, a composite of fact and fiction that was to be analyzed just as one would study any ancient literature. This approach to the Bible came to be known as higher criticism.

During the nineteenth and twentieth centuries, various patterns of response countered biblical criticism. One response was the resurgence of *pietism*, a concerted effort to retreat from the chaos and complexity of modernity to a simpler, less rational approach, where scripture was encountered primarily through one's heart. A second response was that of Protestant *fundamentalism*, which countered modernism by reiterating supernaturalism and the inerrancy of scripture. Fundamentalism was joined by Pentecostalism and evangelicalism, movements that likewise embraced conservative biblicism. A third response, *liberalism*, stressed morality in religion and gave precedence to reason over supernaturalism. Liberalism attempted to redefine Christian tradition in such a way as to engage modernity directly. Embracing the discoveries of higher criticism, liberals replaced literalistic approaches to scripture with moral ones. A fourth response, that of *Roman Catholicism*, accepted religious pluralism and modern biblical criticism while encouraging Catholic laity to engage more directly with scripture, arguing that the Catholic Church was the ultimate interpreter of scripture, with the help of the Holy Spirit.

A Method for Studying the Bible

All literature invites interpretation; all important literature demands it. This is particularly true of scripture, its truth claims fraught with meaning and therefore open to investigation.

There is no such thing as a noninterpretive reading of the Bible. Reading the stories of creation or the stories of Jesus' birth literally involves an interpretive decision equally as much as does the decision to read them metaphorically. When we speak of meaning in relation to a biblical text, five levels come to mind: (1) what the divine author intended (while this concern is primary for conservative readers, it applies indirectly to all who read the Bible as scripture); (2) what the human author intended (this concern should be important to all readers, conservative, moderate, and liberal alike); (3) how biblical scholars and theologians interpret a particular passage or verse (their views, both ancient and modern, are readily available in commentaries, handbooks, Study Bibles, and other interpretive aids. While it is important to recognize the bias or perspective of one's resources, those interested in breadth of insight should consult works from across the denominational and theological spectrum); (4) how leaders in one's church or denomination interpret a particular passage or verse; and finally, (5) what the text means to you. While this final level is indispensable, we should not arrive at it quickly. Without the corrective of the other levels, this approach to the Bible can result in as many meanings as it has readers. This postmodern approach, based on the belief that "the meaning of a text is what it means to me," lacks hermeneutical validity.

We who read the Bible need assistance, a method to help us discern how to hear and value its various voices. When we read scripture, we encounter historical, linguistic, social, and cultural gaps between the ancient and modern worlds, barriers we must overcome if we are to understanding the original meaning of the text. In addition, each of us approaches the text with some preunderstanding of the subject. Those who read the Bible only from the perspective of their immediate personal circumstances, who forget that the passage was originally written for someone else, can easily misunderstand what the text says. We all do this on occasion, but some, seemingly unaware, do so to an extreme.

The Bible, viewed as God's Word, is said to provide unchanging values and eternal commandments. As scripture, the Bible holds answers to life's toughest questions: "Where did we come from? "Why are we here?" and "How will everything end?" Yet the Bible is also a book of bizarre events and strange mysteries, with references to angels and demons, giants and dragons, rivers turning to blood, fire and brimstone raining down on cities, ax-heads floating, people walking on water, and dead people coming back to life.

Also strange are certain commands in the Bible, such as offering animal sacrifices to the Lord, not eating foods like pork and shellfish, not wearing clothing made of more than one material, not tattooing one's body, and doing no work on Saturday. Even in the New Testament people are told to wash one another's feet, to sell everything they have and give the money to the poor, and to pluck out their eye or cut off their hand if they cause you to sin. Women are told to cover their heads with a veil, not to cut their hair or wear pearls or gold jewelry, and to keep quiet in church. Are these cultural matters that no longer apply? If so, what about passages that promote celibacy, discourage marriage, or forbid greed and homosexual behavior? Are these cultural as well? To navigate these challenging waters we need a method (a consistent approach that can be used on any passage), hermeneutical principles, and regular practice. The process of interpreting the

Bible involves building a bridge over a chasm. We are separated from the biblical audience by linguistic, historical, social, and cultural gaps, differences that separate us from the text and that often prohibit us from grasping the meaning of the text. To span this chasm we must erect two pylons, one on either side of the gorge. The first pylon represents *the descriptive task* (discerning what a text *meant* to the original audience), and the second pylon represents *the application task* (discerning what a text *means* to me, in my current situation).

The method I use in biblical study and recommend to my students involves three stages: *exegesis* (what a text *meant* to the original audience; in this phase the exegete [the person studying the Bible] is asked to bring out of the text its natural, intended meaning.), *synthesis* (where one asks particular questions of the text, gathering and surveying, in an historically integrated form, the fruits of exegesis into a meaningful whole), and *application* (what a text *means* to you the reader and to your religious community).[4]

The Canonical Process

Most religious communities have a list of scriptures they consider binding or authoritative. Such a collection is often called a "canon," a concept derived from a Greek word meaning "measuring device" or "ruler." As applied to religious literature, it refers to the rule or standard of authority for belief and practice. Arriving at a definitive canon or binding list of scriptures involves judging the authenticity, doctrinal soundness, and communal acceptance of texts. While Jews and Christians have a "closed" canon, meaning that no books may be added or deleted from that official collection of writings, this does not mean that their religious communities always agree about which books they include in their respective canons, the form of those books, or the order in which those books occur.

By the start of the first century AD, when Christianity emerged, most Jews subscribed to the special authority of the Torah. Not all accepted the authority of the Prophets (for example the Sadducees did not), but most mainline Jews, including the Pharisees, certainly did. Jesus is said to have quoted from some of these books, as did Paul and other New Testament authors, so we can assume that all accepted them as authoritative. The third part, the Writings, was not yet complete in the first century, but one of its major components, the book of Psalms, was already in use in synagogue

---

4. This topic is explored more fully in *Securing Life*, 58–60.

worship. Indeed, this book was so important that the third part of the Jewish canon could be referred to simply as "the Psalms." This usage is found in Luke's Gospel, from the late first century, which refers to "the Law of Moses, the Prophets, and the Psalms" (Luke 24:44).

It should come as no surprise that a faith firmly anchored in the sacred texts of its parent religion would develop scriptures of its own. Christians did develop their own scriptures, but not immediately. The first generation proclaimed its message almost exclusively by word of mouth and saw no pressing need to assemble its own sacred tradition, since it expected Christ to return momentarily. As the expected return of Christ was delayed and as the number of believers continued to expand, the need for written documents became manifest. With the passing away of the first generation of Christians, the need arose to preserve those crucial stories and lessons that had given shape to their community; continuity and order were at stake.

Near the end of the first century AD, Christians were citing Jesus' words and calling them "scripture" (see 1 Tim. 5:18). Furthermore, some of Jesus' followers, such as the apostle Paul, understood themselves to be authoritative spokespersons for the truth (Gal. 1:8–12). Paul's letters, written occasionally to specific congregations and individuals, were reverently saved and shared with Christians in other places. Shortly thereafter they began to assume the authority of scripture, at least among some Christians (2 Pet. 3:16). In fact, Paul's authority was becoming so significant that documents written by others were being ascribed to him (see 2 Thess. 2:2; also the Pastoral Epistles and other disputed letters including Hebrews, which the King James Bible and some Bibles still attribute to Paul). In the next century a host of additional gospels, epistles, and apocalypses appeared, vying for authenticity. The author of Luke's Gospel openly admits that "many writers" had preceded him in the attempt to "draw up an account of the things that have happened among us" (Luke 1:1).

By the third century, more than twenty gospels were in circulation, all claiming, like the Gospel of Peter or the Gospel of Philip, apostolic derivation. Notable among them was the Gospel of Thomas, consisting exclusively of isolated saying attributed to Jesus, some of them said to be older than Mark's Gospel. The abundance of gospels was due mostly to the growth of "gnostic" sects within Christianity, especially in the second century. The vast majority of gnostics were "dualists," believing that human beings were spiritual entities trapped in an evil material world, and that they could be freed, or saved, only through secret knowledge. They shared in common a tendency to produce texts that claimed to distill new revelation. It is no coincidence that the first lists of scripture began to appear among orthodox scholars and theologians shortly after the emergence of gnostic sects. While many gnostic writings were deemed "heretical" (i.e. "false") early on, it is striking that the official canon of twenty-seven book was not finalized until the fourth century.

The process that led to the formation of the Christian canon is complex but fascinating. The four Gospels now found in the New Testament, together with the other canonical writings, may have been produced by diverse, even antithetical communities, but all were viewed to be sufficiently orthodox to make the final cut. However, during the second, third, and fourth centuries, Christians continued to debate the acceptability of certain writings. The arguments centered on three criteria:

- *Apostolicity*: the book in question had to have derived from the initial community of Jesus and his disciples.

- *Orthodoxy*; the book in question had to be valued as inspired and revelatory, that is, as derived directly from God and hence harmonious with the rest of the New Testament.

- *Catholicity*; the book in question had to be accepted and used by a wide range of communities, especially those considered authoritative or apostolic.

At first a local church would have only a few apostolic letters and perhaps one or two Gospels. During the course of the second century most churches came to possess and acknowledge a canon that included the present four Gospels, the Acts, thirteen letters attributed to Paul, 1 Peter, and 1 John. Seven books still lacked general recognition: Hebrews, James, 2 Peter, 2 and 3 John, Jude, and Revelation. On the other hand, certain Christian writings, such as the first letter of Clement, the letter of Barnabas, the Shepherd of Hermas, and the Didache, were accepted as authoritative by several ecclesiastical writers, though rejected by the majority.

Paradoxically, Marcion (c. 140), a heretical Christian preacher in Rome, was responsible for the first canon of the New Testament. Unable to reconcile the Old Testament's portrayal of God as violent and vengeful with the New Testament's portrayal of God as good and loving, he created a restrictive canon that excluded all of the Old Testament and any Christian literature that had Jewish overtones. Marcion's teaching prompted a hearing before other clergy in Rome that resulted in his condemnation in

144. Soon afterward, other church leaders began to form their own canons or lists of approved books. The most famous of these was the Muratorian Canon, dated to the church at Rome circa 190. It included the four Gospels, the Acts of the Apostles, thirteen letters attributed to Paul, Jude, and 1 and 2 John, as well some books that were later excluded, including the Apocalypse of Peter and the Wisdom of Solomon. What is unusual about the latter is that despite being a Jewish work, written prior to the birth of Christianity (in the first century BC), it was listed as a Christian text.

Strangely, the development of a definitive canon of scripture took orthodox Christians nearly four centuries to complete. The earliest surviving list to include all twenty-seven books now known as the New Testament is from the year 367, appearing in an Easter letter written by Athanasius, bishop of Alexandria, to congregations in the eastern section of the church. In the West, the twenty-seven books of the New Testament were accepted at the subsequent councils of Hippo (393) and Carthage (397).

Story Theology

In *Securing Life*, my textbook on the Bible, I addressed the seemingly perplexing question about why the Bible seems to be interpreted and applied so differently by its readers, often due to cultural, sexual, racial, social, and geographical factors. I also pondered why the Bible seem to have a conserving effect on conservative readers, a tempering effect on moderate readers, and a liberating effect on liberal readers. The answer, I suggested, was attributable to four factors, including (1) the tendency to read into the text one's own interests, bias, or meaning (what scholars call "eisegesis"); (2) selective reading of passages that support one's point of view while avoiding passages that challenge cherished beliefs; (3) the polyvalence of scripture (namely, that biblical texts bear multiple layers of meaning); and (4) the nature and depth of one's faith journey and perspective. To these we need to add another reason, (5) the centrality of "story" in Jewish and Christian scriptures.

In our effort to see the significance of scripture, we are greatly aided by this relatively recent emphasis in biblical and theological scholarship. In the 1970s and 1980s, story theology called attention to the centrality of "story" in Jewish and Christian scriptures. This theme can be seen in three features of the Bible: (1) the narrative framework of the Bible as a whole, which on a grand scale can be considered as a single story beginning with paradise lost in the opening chapters of Genesis and concluding with the vision of paradise restored in the book of Revelation; (2) the presence of literally hundreds of individual stories in the Bible; and (3) finally, the centrality in scripture of a small number of "macro-stories"—the primary sources of the religious imagination and life of ancient Israel and the early Christian community.[5]

Story theology not only emphasizes the centrality of story in the biblical tradition, but also criticizes much of Christian theology and modern historical scholarship for having obscured this feature. Theology has typically focused on extracting a core of meaning from a story, which is then expressed conceptually. The story as story is lost. Modern historical study of the Bible has also deemphasized the story, either by searching for the underlying history or by an analytical approach that often loses the story by focusing on its fragments. In both cases, the story as story disappears.

Story theology seeks to recapture the narrative character of scripture. Though it is a recent movement, its approach is very ancient, for the Bible largely originated in story. The story of Israel originated in and was carried by storytelling, as were the Gospels, their traditions about Jesus having been transmitted as stories long before they became texts.

As a genre, religious stories function in a particular way. Unlike religious laws, which address behavior, and unlike theology and doctrine, which address understanding and belief, stories appeal to the imagination. The great stories of the Bible model the religious life. And it is with life, rather than belief, that we are here concerned.

At the heart of scripture lie three macro-stories that have shaped the Old Testament as a whole and have imaged our understanding of Jesus and the religious life in a particular way. Two of the stories are grounded in the history of ancient Israel: the story of the exodus from Egypt and the story of the exile and return from Babylon. The third, the priestly story, is grounded in an institution, namely, the temple, priesthood, and sacrifice. As the three formational stories of the Hebrew Bible, they shaped the religious imagination and understanding of both ancient Israel and the early Christian movement.

1. The *exodus story* is essentially a story of bondage, liberation, journey, and destination. For the slaves, life in Egypt is marked by oppression. The story moves through the plagues and the liberation itself, but does

5. The following is adapted from Borg, *Meeting Jesus Again*, 119–37.

not end with leaving Egypt. Liberation frees the people from the lordship of Pharaoh by transporting them to a transitional phase in their journey: the wilderness sojourn. That phase lasts forty years, but the destination is the Promised Land.

2. Like the exodus story, the *story of exile and return* is grounded in a historical experience, when, after Jerusalem was destroyed by Babylon in 587 BC, many of the Jewish survivors were forced into exile in Babylon. There they lived as refugees for some fifty years, separated from their homeland and under oppression. Next to the exodus, this experience was the most important historical event shaping the life and religious imagination of the Jewish people.

3. The third story, the *priestly story*, is grounded in an institution. Within this story, the priest is the mediator who makes us right with God by offering sacrifice on our behalf. Unlike the previous stories, this one leads to a different image of the religious life. It is not primarily a story of bondage, exile, and journey, but a story of sin, guilt, sacrifice, and forgiveness.

All three stories shape the message of Jesus, the New Testament, and subsequent Christian theology, but only one of them—the priestly story—came to dominate the popular understanding of Jesus and the Christian life to the present day. Despite the power and positive meaning in this model, suggestive of Jesus' love and forgiveness, this image, when it becomes isolated from the others or the dominant understanding of religious life, can produce severe distortions: (1) it leads to a static understanding of the Christian life, making it into a repeated vicious cycle of sin, guilt, and forgiveness; (2) it creates a passive understanding of culture and of the Christian life, thereby losing the sense of life as a process of spiritual transformation; (3) it leads to an understanding of Christianity as primarily a religion of the afterlife, emphasizing belief now for the sake of salvation later; (4) it presents God primarily as lawgiver and judge, picturing God's love as conditional and placing grace within a system of requirements; (5) this story has merit when understood metaphorically, but taken literally, it seems nonsensical; (6) this story works only when people feel guilt, which should not be the central issue in our lives.[6]

The macro-stories, when taken together, are holistic. They share four powerful elements:

---

6. Ibid., 130–31.

- All understand something profound about the human condition, that life involves suffering and alienation.
- All make powerful affirmations about God, portraying God as intimately involved with human life.
- All are stories of hope, new beginnings, and new possibilities.
- All are stories of a journey. This includes the priestly story, for taken in context with the others, the priestly story means that God accepts us just as we are, whatever our place on the journey.

These stories, taken from the Hebrew scriptures, have powerful application in Christianity as well. In addition, the New Testament has a journey story of its own, that of discipleship. The initial clue is the meaning of the word "disciple," which does not mean to be "a pupil of a teacher," but rather a "follower after somebody." Discipleship in the New Testament, of course, is a journeying with Jesus. To follow Jesus means being on the road with him; it means undertaking the journey from the life of conventional wisdom to the alternative wisdom of life in the Spirit. Journeying with Jesus can involve denying him, even betraying him. Journeying with Jesus also means to be in a community, to become part of the alternative community of Jesus. And discipleship involves becoming compassionate, compassion being the defining mark of the follower of Jesus. Compassion is the fruit of life in the Spirit and the ethos of the community of Jesus. This understanding, unlike the conventional moralistic images of the Christian life, presents a transformist, dynamic understanding of the Christian life, where everything old passes away and where everything new becomes better (2 Cor. 5:17).

The Bible in the Postcritical Paradigm

The Bible represents the heart of the Christian tradition, providing Christians their identity, their sacred story. Despite its formational nature, the Bible has become a stumbling block for many Christians today. In particular, many are leaving the church because the Precritical Paradigm's way of reading the Bible—with its emphasis on biblical infallibility, historical factuality, and moral and doctrinal absolutes—cease to make sense to them.

The Postcritical Paradigm provides an alternative to biblical literalism. Utilizing three adjectives—*historical*, *metaphorical*, and *sacramental*—it describes how scripture should be understood. These three approaches apply as well to the creeds and other normative Christian teachings.[7]

1. To speak of *the Bible as a historical product* is to see that it is a human product, not a divine product. Not "absolute truth" but relatively and culturally conditioned, the Bible uses the language and concepts of the cultures in which it took shape. It tells us how our spiritual ancestors saw things, not how God sees things. The Bible is not verbally inspired, since the emphasis is not upon words inspired by God but on people moved by their experience of God.

For the Postcritical Paradigm, describing the Bible as sacred scripture and therefore as "holy" is to value the historical process known as canonization. The documents that make up the Bible were not "sacred" when they were written, but over time were declared sacred, meaning that they became the most important documents for that community, providing its foundation and shaping its identity.

2. Much of the language of the Bible is metaphorical: one-third of the Old Testament is poetry or semi-poetical literature. To speak of *the Bible as metaphor* is to emphasize that this language should not be interpreted literally. Metaphor does not mean that the Bible is not true, but rather that it is not primarily concerned with facticity. The Bible does contain history, but even when a text contains historical memory, its meaning is more than (not less than) literal. For example, although the exile in Babylon in the sixth century BC really happened, the way the story is told gives it a more than historical meaning. As we noted earlier, it became a metaphorical narrative of exile and return, providing images of the human condition and its remedy. In other cases, as the Genesis stories of creation, there may be little or no historical factuality. Though these stories are not literally factual, they are profoundly true.

Because the Gospels combine memory and metaphor, some of these accounts, when literalized, become literally incredible. The story of Jesus changing water into wine at the wedding in Cana (John 2:1–11) illustrates the point. A literal reading of the story emphasizes the spectacular event as a sign of Jesus's identity, "proof" that he was divine. A metaphorical reading of this story yields a different meaning. It notes the story's literary context in John's Gospel as the opening scene of the public activity of Jesus. It seems to be John's way of saying: "Here in a nutshell is what the story of Jesus is about."

---

7. The following points are adapted from Borg, ibid., 43–60.

The story begins: "On the third day, there was a wedding." The phrase "on the third day" evokes the Easter story at the end of the Gospel. The imagery of a wedding banquet helps us view the ministry of Jesus as a celebration at which the wine never runs out and the best is saved for last. Here we have a pointer to the sacramental nature of the Christian life and to the belief that Jesus is God's best.

A metaphorical reading of the Gospels provides rich meaning for Christians in all times and places; a literal reading misses all of this, emphasizing belief in the miraculous elements rather than on its meaning for a life of faith. Metaphorical language is *a way of seeing*. To apply this to the Bible means that in addition to its metaphorical language and metaphorical narratives, the Bible as a whole may be thought of as a "giant" metaphor. "Thus the point is not to believe in the Bible—but to see our lives with God through it."[8]

3. To speak of *the Bible as sacrament* is to say that it mediates the sacred. If a sacrament is a physical vehicle or vessel for the Spirit, the Bible is sacrament in the sense that it is a visible human product whereby God becomes present to us.

For the Postcritical Paradigm, "the Bible—human in origin, sacred in status and function—is both metaphor and sacrament. As metaphor, it is a way of seeing—a way of seeing God and our life with God. As sacrament, it is a way that God speaks to us and comes to us."[9] The Bible is a two-way bridge, a path to the divine and a way to connect to our deepest self. Like a backboard in the game of basketball, scripture is a means to an end, not an end in itself.

Going Deeper: Reflection for Participants

1. In your estimation, why should we read the Bible? Does our motivation matter?

2. What do Christians generally mean when they say that the Bible is "holy"? Does the word "sacred" necessarily imply anything supernatural about the origin or nature of scripture? Explain your answer.

---

8. Ibid., 57.
9. Ibid., 59.

3. How important is genre to your reading of the Bible? What difference should genre make in our study of scripture?

4. Evaluate the author's statement that "when conservative Christians quote scripture to authenticate its own inspiration, they practice circular reasoning, always questionable."

5. Discuss the merits of literalist and contextualist views of biblical inspiration, and how the notion of "inspired process" expands your understanding of biblical inspiration.

6. Of the three criteria for determining the acceptance of New Testament writings into the canon, which to you is most convincing: apostolicity, orthodoxy, or catholicity? Explain your answer.

7. Do you agree with the intentions, conclusions, and methodology implied in "story theology"? What weaknesses or problems do you find in such an approach to scripture? What merits or benefits do you find in this approach?

8. What lessons from the Exodus Story can you learn about bondage in your own life? What would liberation from such bondage look and feel like?

9. What lessons from the Story of Exile and Return can you learn about your own human condition? What would return from such exile look and feel like?

10. What lessons from the Priestly Story can you learn about sin and forgiveness in your own life? Identify a particular sin in your life and describe what forgiveness from that sin might look and feel like.

11. In your estimation, what is the primary insight gained from this session?

Session 7

Rethinking Creation
Divine Act or Ongoing Process?

Getting Started

Homework Assignment: Answer the following question, writing your answer in your journal. Be prepared to share your views with others in the class. 1. Is creation an act of divine fiat in the past, an ongoing evolutionary process, or somehow both? Support your answer.

Gaining Momentum

As previously stated, starting theological discussions with the Spirit model rather than the monarchical model of God affects the meaning of a number of central Christian teachings. It changes the framework by which we view reality. In this session we will explore how the Spirit model transforms our understanding of the doctrine of creation.

According to the monarchical model, God's creation of the world is understood as an event in the distant past involving the creation of a universe separate from God. The Spirit model depicts God's creation as an ongoing activity: in every moment God as Spirit (as the nonmaterial "ground" of all that is) is bringing the universe into existence.

The Doctrine of Creation

The doctrine of creation is central to all biblical faith traditions. This doctrine affirms that God created all things, meaning that the world and everything in it depends on God for its existence. Whereas prominent Greek thinkers such as Plato and Aristotle virtually ignored origins, accepting the explanation that matter, and therefore the world, was eternal, the Bible presents an external force that created and continually sustains the cosmos.

In the Bible, however, the doctrine of creation does not stand alone but depends upon and elaborates on the redemptive activity of God in history. In the Old Testament, creation is viewed in the light of Israel's covenant faith; in the New Testament, creation is viewed in the light of Jesus Christ and the "new creation" that through him became a historical reality. In both Testaments, the doctrine emphasizes the sovereignty of God, the goodness of creation (that the cosmos and everything in it is characterized by design, that is, by a divinely decreed order), the supreme position of honor and responsibility that God has given to human beings, and the divine purpose that undergirds and controls history from its beginning to its consummation.

Creation faith, particularly as affirmed in the historic creeds of Christianity, represents a repudiation of metaphysical dualism, which suggests that the created world is evil, and a repudiation of metaphysical randomness, which suggests that life is essentially meaningless. Creation faith is what Christians overwhelmingly affirm when they profess: "I believe in God the Father almighty, maker of heaven and earth."

Keys to Interpreting the Biblical Doctrine of Creation

As we examine the stories in Genesis 1–11, passages central to the biblical doctrine of creation, we need to consider several general observations.

1. *Literary Sources*: The first observation concerns the literary sources said to underlie the text. Scholars accept that Genesis 1–11 come from two different traditions, commonly called the Yahwist (J) and the Priestly Writer (P), which were combined, expanded, and redacted over time, a process completed around 400 BC by Ezra, an influential scribe called "the founder of Judaism." The J material (found in Genesis 2:4b—4:26; 11:1–9; in parts of the flood narrative; and in the genealogies) is taken to be earlier. This source, said to represent a critique of royal autonomy (perhaps Solomonic),

may be viewed as a polemic against the willful pride of the creature who will not live in harmony with the creator but craves autonomy (see Gen. 3:5 and 11:6). The P source, commonly dated to the Babylonian exile (587–539 BC), deals with the problem of hopelessness. This tradition is found in Genesis 1:1—2:4a; in parts of the flood narrative; and in the genealogies. While the former tradition is concerned with prideful self-assertion, the latter deals with despair. Against despair, it asserts not only humanness in the image of God (1:26), but the endurance of this image even after the expulsion from the garden (5:1) and after the flood (9:6). These two literary sources and their competing theological agendas live in uneasy tension.

2. *Symmetrical Structure*: While the structure of Genesis 1–11 is difficult and admits various interpretations, scholars have detected various symmetrical correlations in this unit, including:

- Two basic creation accounts: pre-flood (1:1—2:24) and post-flood (9:1–17).
- Two stories of disobedience: pre-flood (6:1–4) and post-flood (9:18–28).
- Two genealogies of continuity: pre-flood (5:1–32) and post-flood (10:1–32; 11:10–29).
- Two major traditions of sin and judgment: pre-flood (3:1—4:16) and post-flood (11:1–9).[1]

According to this interpretation, the carefully structured flood narrative stands at the center, having as its main counterpoint the creation of the world in chapter 1. These two narratives provide the main dynamic of the unit: creation; uncreation; new creation. Because Genesis 1–11 as presently shaped ends with the genealogy of Abraham, Genesis 12:1–4 completes the symmetry, its theme of promise the counterpart of chapter 1.

3. *View of History*: Unlike the cyclical pattern of nature, which guided both agrarian and nomadic peoples in antiquity, the biblical authors maintained a linear view of history, bracketed by a beginning and an end. Unlike their neighbors, who viewed life as repetitive, biblical writers viewed history as purposive. The very idea of purpose, however, implies both the initiation of purpose (a beginning) and the attainment of purpose (an end). Purposive history moves forward in the direction of the realization of a goal. Therefore, the Bible deals with "first things," that is, with God's

1. Brueggemann, *Genesis*, 14–22.

initiation of the drama of human history, as well as "last things," the conclusion of the historical drama in the purpose of God. "Beginning and end are the terminal points of an interpretation of history which measures time according to the realization of God's purpose."[2] In other words, the biblical drama, both at the beginning and the end, is bounded by and part of the incomprehensible mystery of "eternity," that is, by "God's Time." Clearly, we are dealing here with an interpretation of history that lies beyond the scope of science.

Accordingly, it is wrong to suppose that the biblical authors were primitive scientists who speculated on the origin and dissolution of nature. The very fact that Genesis includes two strikingly different accounts of creation indicates that the authors of the Pentateuch were concerned with the religious meaning of the stories, not with scientific or even consistent accounts of the way nature evolves. When the P writer arranges his story into six creative days, he is not doing so for historical or scientific reasons but for a religious one, namely, to show the sanctity of the Jewish Sabbath. The pattern: six days God "labored" and on the seventh day God "rested" also emphasizes that from the very beginning, God established a pattern to guide Israel's national life.

4. *Universality of Scope*: The fourth observation concerns the universal scope present in the biblical depiction of creation. These stories not only place history within God's timespan, but they emphasize that the whole creation is included within God's redemptive purpose. The biblical stories of the beginning and the end have a universal range of interest; they concern all humanity and not merely Israel narrowly. In particular, the stories of Genesis 1–11 indicate that the God of Abraham, Isaac, and Jacob is the God of all nations; the whole human drama having its beginning (and its ending) in the creative Word of God: "And God said . . . And it was so."

5. *The Language of Myth*: The fifth observation concerns the language of creation. The Bible speaks of the eternal boundaries of the human drama metaphorically, in the language of myth. The term "myth," understood literarily, does not refer to something purely fictitious, but rather is a way of thinking that transcends reason. Scholars of religion often use the term "myths" to refer to the central narratives of a religious tradition, insisting that the term does not imply any judgment either for or against the historicity or validity of the narratives.

---

2. Anderson, *Rediscovering the Bible*, 239.

Central religious myths manifest the character of the cosmic order and our relationship to it. Significant in personal and communal life because they endorse particular ways of ordering experience, myths provide exemplary patterns for human actions, individually and communally. Mythology, Karen Armstrong reminds us, "is not about opting out of this world, but about enabling us to live more intensely within it."[3]

The dictionary defines a myth as a story dealing with the actions of the gods, in contrast to a legend, which deals with the actions of humans. This is a helpful distinction, in part because it puts the accent upon divine action. Dismissal of myth and other types of religious symbolism usually rests upon the belief that the meaning of life can be defined by reason, and that truth can be measured by the scientific method. Yet most of us realize that there are areas in which the most important truths have an immeasurable quality, as in the case of falling in love, and that we must turn to poetry, song, and art for the expression of life's deepest experiences.

About one third of the Hebrew Bible is poetry. Awareness of this feature of Israel's liturgical and literary expression is invaluable for reading and interpreting scripture. As artists communicate life's deeper dimension by transforming the things of the everyday world into the language of symbol and imagination, so also the biblical writers use myth and symbol to communicate the faith that human history, as the arena of God's purposive activity, reaches backward and forward into the endless Time of God.

We know that many myths circulated in the ancient world and that this mythology profoundly influenced the biblical tradition. The biblical writers borrowed freely from the common fund of mythology, though purging the myths of their polytheism and other archaic features. The opening chapters of Genesis set human life in a framework of significance and meaning. They portray a world that is good, orderly, and coherent. They picture a God who is free, transcendent, and purposeful. These theological affirmations are conveyed through a dramatic narrative, which assumes a prescientific cosmology. The creation account is the basis for gratitude for the created order, celebrated in the liturgy of ancient psalms and modern prayers and hymns. A view of creation also affects care toward nature and appropriate ways in which to treat the environment.

6. *Creation and Worship*: Analysis destroys myth, just as the beauty of a poem or the mystery of love vanishes when it is dissected. A myth must be viewed in its totality, every part blending into a poetic whole. This is as

---

3. Armstrong, *Short History of Myth*, 3.

true of the Priestly story of creation (Gen. 1:1—2:4a) as of the Yahwist story of the Fall (Gen. 3 1–24), which were intended to be read aloud or heard to be appreciated. The original setting of these passages, widely gleaned in modern times for historical and scientific truths, is not a laboratory or a classroom but rather corporate worship. The setting of the creation-faith within worship is clearly evident in Psalm 24, a three-part liturgy once used during great pilgrimage festivals celebrating Yahweh's kingship. The psalm was undoubtedly used originally in connection with a processional bearing of the Ark of the Covenant into Jerusalem. The opening word of the psalm, which announce that Yahweh is creator, functioned as an introit: "The earth is the Lord's and all that is in it, the world, and those who live in it; for he has founded it on the seas, and established it on the rivers" (24:1–2). The second part, in question-and-response format (24:3–6), is a liturgy for admission to the temple, and the third, an "entrance liturgy" (24:7–10), was sung antiphonally in the presence of the ark, understood to be Yahweh's throne-seat. In this liturgical setting, the function of creation language is to set the stage for praising God. Thus in the book of Psalms, known as the hymnbook of Judaism, the affirmation that God is the creator is a call to worship.

In the 1920s, when a storm of controversy broke out in the United States over the doctrine of evolution, people passionately took sides in the "science versus religion" battle, some attempting to demonstrate that the biblical doctrine of creation is good science and others rejecting it as bad science. That conflict continues today between evolutionists (theistic and atheistic) and anti-evolutionists like Young Earth Creationists and Intelligent Design proponents. Fortunately, as many now realize, the conflict resulted from a failure to understand the intention of Israel's language of worship.

The word "creation" is neither scientific or philosophical; rather it is theological, a language whose affirmations should not be confused with statements made in the context of secular or scientific thought. In the Bible, the announcement that God is the creator primarily concerns the source and basis of life's meaning. Negatively, it counters the notion that the world is at our disposal, to use or misuse as we please. To understand the creation stories at the beginning of the Bible we ought to divest our minds of scientific and philosophical preconceptions and begin with the Psalms, which praise God as the creator. While the position of the Priestly story of creation is the opening of a cosmic drama, the prelude of the story of God's special dealings with humanity, the form of the story suggests that it was shaped by liturgical usage over a period of many generations, perhaps in connection with one of the great pilgrimage festivals of Israel, and thus it is told confessionally to glorify the God of Israel.

This leads to an important point. When creation-faith is interpreted within the context of worship, there is a tendency to shift the accent from creation as the event at the beginning to a relationship in the present, from the horizontal dimension (the movement of events from beginning to end) to the vertical dimension (the relationship between God and humanity). In our time, the existentialist interpretation of creation has found wide support. In his commentary on Genesis 1–11, Alan Richardson suggests that we consider these stories as "parables," to be read as poetry, not prose. The parables of Genesis, he says, contain a special kind of truth: "not the truth with which history and geography, astronomy and geology, deal; it is not the literal truth of the actual observation of measurable things and events; it is ultimate truth, the truth which can be grasped only by the imagination, and which can be expressed by image and symbolism."[4] Such truth, "the truth of religious awareness," cannot be expressed in philosophical, theological, or psychological terms, for that would be to depersonalize it. You are Adam, I am Eve; this is our story!

Psalm 8, related to the Priestly creation account in Genesis 1, is an eloquent witness to the meaning of creation-faith in the liturgy of Israel's worship. This hymn begins and ends with an exclamation of praise to God's glory and majesty, which, to the eye of faith, are evident in nature. The psalmist knows that we sometimes take this world for granted, and yet he knows too that praise is the sign that we are alive, that we are fully human. Creation-faith focuses upon the relationship between God and humanity: "When I look at your heavens, the work of your fingers, the moon and the stars that you have established, what are human beings that you are mindful of them, mortals that you care for them?" (Ps. 8:3–4). It is not simply that humans, in contrast to God, are finite. As the book of Ecclesiastes shows, the awareness of the gulf fixed between creature and creator can prompt a feeling of futility and desolation (Eccl. 1:12–14; 3:16–22; 6:1–2). Rather, creation-faith provides context for understanding existence, the awareness that our relationship with God is one of incomprehensible grace. As we see also in the Priestly creation story, where humans are said to be created "in the image of God" (Gen. 1:27), praise rises to a climax as the psalmist

---

4. Richardson, *Genesis I-XI*, 30.

draws upon the old cultic tradition: "You have made [humans] a little lower than God, and crowned them with glory and honor. You have given them dominion over the works of your hands; you have put all things under their feet" (Ps. 8:5–6).

7. *Stewardship*:[5] Our final observation concerns the creation mandates given to humans in Genesis 1:28—2:3. Though the word "covenant" does not appear in the creation narrative, theologians speak of God's relation with Adam and Eve prior to their departure from the Garden as the covenant of creation. Like God's call (election) of Abraham, basic to the covenant of creation is the cultural mandate God gives to Adam and Eve, whereby they are to be God's servants on earth. Unlike the *Enuma Elish* (the Babylonian creation account), where humans are depicted as servile by nature, creating society to protect themselves from capricious gods, Genesis 1 depicts humans as divine image-bearers, vice-regents with God, and God institutes creation ordinances for their wellbeing. These ordinances include family (procreation and marriage; 1:28), labor (work is not a curse but a blessing; 1:28), and worship (the Hebrew verb for "rest" [*shabath*], is the basis of the word "Sabbath," the day of rest. As God rests from the labor of creation, so the Sabbath completes the workweek, thereby establishing a pattern of work followed by rest. As this passage suggests, duty and pleasure are complementary, not antithetical; 2:1–3).

The concept of realizing and acting upon one's ordained position as God's co-worker (vice-regent) is called stewardship. The covenant of creation binds all humans to God and to one another. It entails that, as image-bearers, humans are to reflect God's concern for all of life. That includes using wealth and property for the benefit of the entire community. The Bible provides many examples of how this occurs, stressing the welfare of the poor (the fatherless, widow, and sojourner; the book of James in the New Testament powerfully summarizes this concept in 1:27: "Religion that is pure and undefiled before God, the Father, is this: to care for orphans and widows in their distress . . ."). In Deuteronomy 24:19–22 God instructs the Israelites to harvest their fields only once a season; what remains is reserved for the needy. Leviticus 23:22 commands farmers not to harvest their land to the borders, but to leave the produce at the edges for the poor. The Bible also contains strict regulations regarding lending practices (Exod. 22:25–27), provides for an impartial judicial process (Deut.

---

5. This segment on stewardship is adapted from Bowne and Currid, "Biblical Society," 160–61 and 166–68.

16:18–20), and for paying the poor and needy worker on the day they earn their hire (Deut. 24:14–15). Partiality and bribery are denounced, and the Hebrews are warned to protect strangers and foreigners in their midst, for God protected them while they were strangers in Egypt (Exod. 22:21–24). As Deuteronomy 16:20 makes clear, the concept of stewardship embodies the principle of justice, and, indirectly, of righteousness and steadfast love: "Justice, and only justice, you shall pursue, so that you may live and occupy the land that the Lord your God is giving you."

The institution of marriage stands at the center of biblical society. In ancient Israel and among its neighbors, marriage was a religious affair, a transaction between two families bound by a covenant agreement and sealed with an exchange of gifts. The Israelites viewed marriage as a religious rite because God had ordained marriage at the creation: "Therefore a man leaves his father and his mother and clings to his wife, and they become one flesh" (Gen. 2:24). Though the Israelite system of marriage recognized the practice of polygamy and placed no restrictions on the number of wives a man could have (provided he could financially support them), the ideal was unmistakably monogamous marriage (Gen. 2:24).

The belief that marriage was ordained by God and existed under the covenant illustrates further the Hebrew conviction that all of life lies under God's sovereignty. Furthermore, the Old Testament upholds the sanctity of marriage as a religious ritual by frequently using marriage as a metaphor to depict the relationship between God and the Hebrew nation.

As we examine the biblical covenant of creation, particularly its universality, we need to take inventory. How well are human beings doing in the area of stewardship? If Christians fail to lead the way in justice, righteousness, compassion, and stewardship, does God have a back-up plan?

Science and Religion: Toward an Open Universe

In many ways, a sharp and ever-widening gulf characterizes the relationship between Christian scholars and traditional lay persons. The chasm is attributed to several factors, including the assumptions and conclusions of modern scholarship as well as the convictions and needs of parishioners. Scholars seek factual knowledge, whereas laypersons seek inspiration and reassurance. Not all parishioners, of course, are traditionalists, and not all scholars are progressive or open to new ways of thinking about their faith.

Rethinking Creation

As we noticed earlier (see Session 4), one's view of God affects the meaning of such central Christians teachings as scripture, sin, salvation, evil, and the role of the church, and when our view of God changes from a monarchical to a Spirit model, creation looks different as well. According to the monarchical model, God's creation of the world is understood as an event in the distant past involving the creation of a universe separate from God. The Spirit model depicts God's creation as ongoing: in every moment God as Spirit (as the nonmaterial "ground" of all that is) is bringing the universe into existence.

Economist E. F. Schumacher, author of *Small Is Beautiful*, believed there are two places to find wisdom: in nature and in religious traditions. To seek wisdom in nature one should look to science, to those who love nature enough to study it. Because science explores nature, it can be a powerful source of wisdom. In most developed cultures, religion and science have teamed to offer a cosmic story that allows people to understand their universe, find meaning in it, and live out their lives with purpose. In the West, however, religion and science have been at odds since the seventeenth century. This split has been disastrous: religion has become privatized and science a tool of technology. As philosopher Alfred North Whitehead wrote: "Religion is tending to degenerate into a decent formula wherewith to embellish a comfortable life . . . Religion will not regain its old power until it can face change in the same spirit as does science."[6] To recover the wisdom embedded in religious traditions, we must abandon unhelpful religious traditions. In the words of Meister Eckhart, the profound mystical theologian of the West: "Only those who dare to let go can dare to reenter."

In the past four centuries, remarkable changes have occurred in the field of science, including what is known about the motion of the heavens, elementary substances, and origins of the cosmos and of the human race. New conceptions of the cosmos led to new views concerning God and God's relation with the world. Modern Christians essentially regard science as a good gift and appreciate its benefits. Yet when science addresses religious concerns such as human origins or divine sovereignty, many Christians feel they need to choose between the competing claims of religion and science. In such situations, conventional Christians favor the claims of religion.

Twenty-first-century cosmogonies present several alternatives, namely the choice between a universe closed to influences from God and a

---

6. Whitehead, *Science and the Modern World*, 188–89.

universe open to influences from God.[7] If the universe is held to be closed in the sense proposed by scientific materialists, then what is observable is solely the result of "natural laws" upon pre-existent matter and/or energy. No guidance or design is needed. The other major alternative is that the universe is open to God's influences, which may be overt or subtle.

Under the alternative of an open universe, various options exist, differing principally on how one understands the role of God during the creative process:

1. *Creationism* affirms the biblical view that God created the world in the manner described in the first chapter of Genesis. Proponents of this view disagree over the precise nature and duration of the creation. Three options exist, each affirming the notion of biblical inspiration: (a) the *literal chronological view* interprets the Hebrew word *yom* (translated "day") in Genesis 1 as a literal twenty-four period. In addition, each "day" is understood chronologically, so that during the first twenty-four hours of time God created light, in the second day the firmament, and so forth until the completion of creation after six literal days. The Genesis 1 narrative, therefore, is understood simply as history. (b) The *figurative chronological view* interprets the word *yom* figuratively, as an indeterminate length of time. The chronology of the days remains the same, but the days themselves are lengthened. This position, first proposed in the nineteenth century in response to new scientific discoveries regarding the age of the earth, attempts to harmonize geological research and scripture. Exponents of this view argue that the period of six "days" could extend to four billion years or more. (c) The *figurative topical view*, also known as "the framework hypothesis," asserts that Genesis 1 is a literary work using poetic elements to arrange creation by topic, not by sequence or chronology. Thus the order of the Genesis 1 account is figurative, as is the use of the term "day." According to this view, the pattern of six days contains two sets of triads. The first triad (days 1, 2, 3) establishes three spheres or realms, and the second triad (days 4, 5, 6) names various subjects that inhabit those realms. A direct correspondence is portrayed between days 1 and 4, 2 and 5, and 3 and 6. The topical structure of the narrative is as follows:

---

7. A cosmogony is an account of the generation of the universe; it represents a model of history, a hypothesis about the past that cannot be tested by experiment and therefore remains a conjecture.

Spheres	Subjects
Day 1. Light	Day 4. Light Bearers
(Gen. 1:3–5)	(Gen. 1:14–19)
Day 2. Sea, Sky	Day 5. Fish, Birds
(Gen. 1:6–8)	(Gen. 1:20–23)
Day 3. Land, Vegetation	Day 6. Land Animals, Humans
(Gen. 1:9–13)	(Gen. 1:24–31)

Day 7. Sabbath
(Gen. 2:1–4a)

According to this third option, the function of the creation narrative is to help the worshiping community focus on the centrality of the Sabbath and on worship. The text is only secondarily about creation, which unfolds according to a meaningful pattern.

Each view has advantages and disadvantages, but all maintain a high regard for biblical authority. All three views affirm God as the creator and sustainer of the universe.

2. *Theistic evolution* accepts the reality of evolution and posits God's guidance. This view also has two major variants: (a) *progressive creation* holds that God continually directed the course of the cosmos while forming and filling it, making use of and guiding processes designed by God; (b) *theistic macroevolution* maintains that God originally created matter and its laws and later created humans in his image. Except for those two acts of creation, the universe has developed according to secondary causes as though it were a closed system.[8]

The idea of theistic evolution has a long-standing support in the Christian tradition.[9] In his work *On the Literal Meaning of Genesis*, written early in the fifth century, Augustine (354–430) set out to provide a doctrine of creation based on his interpretation of the Genesis creation accounts.

---

8. Rice, "Cosmology of Modern Science," 106–7.

9. The phrase "theistic evolution" is used to characterize the views of a wide range of thinkers. In my estimation the phrase is flawed, in part because "theistic" is a rather pale adjective to refer to the God of Christian faith: it places too much emphasis on the transcendence of God and lacks the depth we examine more fully in this chapter. I am also uncomfortable with the label "creationist" or "creationism" because in the public mind these terms are usually seen as opposed to "evolutionist" or "evolution." Perhaps a better phrase is "evolutionary creation," for it best conveys (1) the belief that the God of biblical faith has empowered the universe and life with the ability to evolve, and (2) the belief that God continuously creates through these evolutionary processes.

Believing that God brought everything into existence in a single moment of creation, he argued that the created order should not be viewed as static, inasmuch as God endowed it with the capacity to develop. Augustine used the image of a dormant seed as an analogy for this process. Within the original created order God embeds seminal principles (*rationes seminales*, meaning "seed-bearing reasons"), which grow and develop at the right time.[10]

Earlier Christian writers noted how Genesis 1 spoke of the earth and the waters "bringing forth" living creatures, concluding that this pointed to God's having endowed the natural order with a capacity to generate living things. Augustine took this idea further, arguing that God inserted into the world dormant powers, which were actualized at appropriate moments through divine providence. Augustine argued that Genesis 1:12 implies that the earth had received the power or capacity to produce things by itself. Where some might think of creation in terms of God's insertion of new kinds of plants and animals ready-made into an already existing world, Augustine rejected this as inconsistent with the overall witness of scripture. Rather, God must be thought of as creating in that very first moment the potencies for all kinds of living things that would come later, including humanity. Augustine believed that God had created a universe designed to develop and evolve.

Augustine was a complex man, and neither he nor his theology was flawless. Nevertheless, he left his followers a legacy by giving them two principles to follow as they plunged into the unknown future: (1) the principle of accommodation and (2) the principle of the integrity of science. No die-hard biblical literalist, Augustine took science very seriously, and his "principle of accommodation" would dominate biblical interpretation in the West until well into the early modern period. Because God had adapted revelation to the cultural norms of the people who had first received it, biblical passages were couched in the cosmology of antiquity and could not be interpreted literally. God had simply accommodated the truths of revelation to the science of the day so that the original audience could understand them. Whenever the literal meaning of scripture clashed with reliable scientific information, Augustine insisted, the interpreter must respect the integrity of science or bring scripture into disrepute. People who engaged in acrimonious debate of religious truth were simply in love with their own opinions and had forgotten the cardinal teaching of the Bible, which was

10. McGrath, *Christian Theology*, 218.

the love of God and neighbor. The exegete must not leave a text until he established "the reign of charity," and if a literal understanding of any biblical passage seemed to teach hatred or discord, the text must be interpreted allegorically and forced to preach love.

The Augustinian option, viewed favorably by evolutionary theists, says that, no matter why things are as they are, the fact is that humans evolved and did so by the will of God, in conjunction, no doubt, with all sorts of random factors. God did not impersonally plan all things beforehand and then let them happen, but God is actively involved in seeing that things occur as they should. The laws and the events, random or not, are God laws and events, their end foreseen and intended by God. Therefore God deserves credit.

There are, of course, costs to the solution, costs that must be paid by any Augustinian. In the first place, the whole question of freedom—particularly the freedom of the human will—is thrown into doubt. Does God control everything to such an extent that things had to happen, no matter what anything in creation wanted or intended? Or does one want to argue that free will came into play only when humans finally appeared?

In the second place, there is the question of evil and pain. Even if we attribute a great deal of evil to the actions of free humans, there still remains natural evil or pain. If God so controls things that humans appeared despite the improbability, then is God also responsible for such things as bad mutations? Is God responsible for those earthquakes and floods and other natural calamities that take so many innocent lives? Making God responsible at one level seems to entail making God responsible at other levels as well.[11]

Many Christians today find it difficult to accept the notion that creation and evolution belong together. The belief that such concepts are opposing and conflicting has become so ingrained in the minds of many that it is hard to conceptualize how the God of the Bible may work out his creative purposes through an evolutionary process. Believers have been taught that they must choose between creation and evolution. However, many distinguished scientists and theologians are inviting us to see that this is a false choice and asking us to consider instead a both/and alternative.

The eminent biologist Theodosius Dobzhansky (1900–1975), who immigrated to the United States from the Soviet Union, did important work in the field of population genetics and was instrumental in the development of the Modern Synthesis of evolutionary theory. He was also a practicing

---

11. Ruse, *Can a Darwinian Be a Christian?*, 91–92.

Russian Orthodox Christian. "It is wrong," he wrote, "to hold creation and evolution as mutually exclusive alternatives. I am a creationist *and* an evolutionist." In his writings he presented a tribute to paleontologist Pierre Teilhard de Chardin, another Christian who embraced evolution and who influenced him spiritually: "There is no doubt at all that Teilhard was a truly and deeply religious man and that Christianity was the cornerstone of his worldview. Moreover, in his worldview science and faith were not segregated in watertight compartments, as they are with so many people. They were harmoniously fitting parts of his worldview. Teilhard was a creationist, but one who understood that the Creation is realized in this world by means of evolution."[12]

Were Dobzhansky and Teilhard the only Christians in the sciences who brought evolution and creation together, one might choose to dismiss them, but in fact they are among many scientists, in the United States and elsewhere, who have done so, including many evangelical Christians. What these men and women are doing is hardly new. Beginning in the thirteenth century, theologians adapted their understanding of creation to the Aristotelian-Ptolemaic model of an earth-centered circular cosmos, so different from the ancient Hebraic model. Later, after struggling with the Copernican and the Newtonian models, theologians eventually found ways to accommodate their thinking to that cosmology as well. The current reflections on God's action in an evolving creation—the universe of Darwin and Einstein—stand very much in this tradition of faith seeking understanding.[13]

Unfortunately, many Christians are unaware of this history. They are also unaware that the work of understanding creation and evolution together flourished in Darwin's day. During the latter half of the nineteenth century many prominent evangelical and Reformed theologians and scientists in both the United Kingdom and North America concluded that evolutionary science is not in conflict with Christian faith in creation.

During the decades following the publication of *The Origin of Species*, Darwin enjoyed the support of many Anglican clergy, including leading educators and theologians. Theologian Aubrey Moore described Darwin as one who, "disguised as a foe, did the work of a friend," for thanks to him Christianity must now understand that "God is everywhere present in

---

12. Dobzhansky, "Biology Makes Sense," 125–29.
13. Schneider, *Science and Faith*, Essay VII: "Theologies of an Evolving Creation."

nature."[14] The prominent Calvinist theologian James Orr (1844–1913) was among many who accepted evolution while disagreeing with some aspects of Darwin's own interpretation of the process: "Assume God—as many devout [Christian] evolutionists do—to be immanent in the evolutionary process, and His intelligence and purpose to be expressed in it; then evolution, so far from conflicting with theism, may become a new and heightened form of the theistic argument. The real impelling force of evolution is now from within."[15]

This re-evaluation of the ancient doctrine of God's immanence in creation became a theme in the writings of biologist Asa Gray (1810–1888) and geologist James Dana (1813–1895). Both were active churchman, committed to traditional Christian doctrine. Gray, America's foremost botanist, was a friend of Darwin's. From his extensive studies of American flora he abandoned separate creation and found in natural selection a convincing explanation for the great variety of plant species. Dana, a leading American geologist, began as a progressive creationist, but came in time to accept evolution, seeing natural selection as a natural law or method that pointed beyond nature to a Lawgiver. Both scholars rejected the notion of evolution as materialistic and aimless. Holding to "a strictly scientific Darwinism," they were convinced that evolution did not contradict belief in design and purpose in nature.

Likewise, thinkers in the Reformed tradition related theology and science in a positive way. These included Presbyterian philosopher James McCosh (1811–1894), who became president of Princeton University in 1868, and Presbyterian theologian Benjamin B. Warfield (1851–1921), a professor at Princeton Seminary. McCosh devoted himself to developing a natural theology that incorporated evolution. Warfield, a highly respected thinker, was an orthodox Calvinist and perhaps in his era the most articulate promoter of biblical inerrancy; yet, he saw no conflict between scripture and science when it came to understanding evolution as an expression of God's creative activity. "I am free to say, for myself," he wrote, "that I do not think there is any general statement in the Bible, or any part of the account of creation, either as given in Gen. I & II, or elsewhere alluded to, that need be opposed to evolution."[16] Warfield could say this because, following Calvin, he held that scripture did not need to be interpreted literally when

---

14. Cited in Peacocke, "Biological Evolution," 357
15. Cited in Livingstone, *Darwin's Forgotten Defenders*, 142.
16. Ibid., 118.

it referred to nature. Furthermore, "the findings of science could be enlisted to help discover proper interpretations of scripture."[17]

Like other theologians sympathetic to evolution, Warfield read deeply in the field and kept abreast of developments. And like his colleagues Gray and Dana he distinguished between "evolution" and "Darwinism," meaning by the latter a wholly materialistic process, and accepted the former while rejecting the latter.

These men were among the most influential of a large number of nineteenth-century churchmen who integrated a scientific understanding of Darwinian evolution with a comprehensive theological worldview anchored in conservative Christianity. It is ironic that at the very time when the discovery of DNA and research in molecular biology were providing much more compelling evidence for evolution, the movement known as Young Earth Creationism and its Intelligent Design variant have persuaded many people in North America that evolution and creation are opposed to one another and that evolution is an atheistic philosophy that leaves no room for God.

Contemporary theology has put forth a variety of new models of God's relationship to the creation, yet all agree on one thing: God is to be understood not as intervening from outside the creation to perform creative acts, but instead as interacting with every creature within the creation itself. As Roman Catholic theologian Denis Edwards puts it, the Triune God "is present to every creature in its being and becoming."[18] God's presence pervades every part and particle of the universe from its beginning in the Big Bang to the emergence of each new living species.

Science and Religion: Three Models

What philosopher Alfred North Whitehead stated in 1925 still holds true today: "When we consider what religion is for mankind, and what science is, it is no exaggeration to say that the future course of history depends upon the decision of this generation as to the relations between them. We have here the two strongest general forces . . . which influence men, and they seem to be set one against the other—the force of our religious

---

17. Noll and Livingstone, "Hodge and Warfield on Science," 64.
18. Edwards, *The God of Evolution*, 32–33.

institutions, and the force of our own impulse to accurate observation and logical deduction."[9]

Examining the spectrum of contemporary views, Roman Catholic theologian John Haught identified three distinct ways in which science and religion can be related to each other:
opposition (conflict), separation (contrast), and engagement (contact).[20]

1. Within the Opposition camp there are several viewpoints, unanimous in their claim that religion and science are irreconcilable and mutually antagonistic in their assessment of which option provides an ultimate explanation of reality. They can be examined under two broad categories: *scientific materialism*, also known as "scientism" (characterized by a mindset in which the scientific method is the only reliable path to knowledge), and *biblical literalism* (characterized by a mindset in which religious faith and scripture always trump evidence). While both represent the opposite ends of the theological spectrum, they share various characteristics in common. Both believe that there are serious conflicts between contemporary science and classical religious beliefs. Both seek knowledge with a sure foundation—that of logic and sense data, on the one hand, that of infallible scripture, on the other. They both claim that science and theology make rival literal statements about the same domain—the history of nature—so that one must choose between them. Both represent a misuse of science. The scientific materialist starts from science but ends up making broad philosophical claims. The biblical literalist moves from theology to make claims about scientific matters. Both fail to respect the differences between the two disciplines. The idea that science is locked in eternal combat with religion is an understandable reaction to the common practice of confusing their respective roles.

2. One way to avoid conflicts between science and religion is to view the two realms as independent and autonomous. Each has its own domain and its characteristic methods. Proponents of the Separation view say there are two jurisdictions and each must tend to its own business and not meddle in the affairs of the other. The task of science is *descriptive*, answering "what," "how," and "what is" questions, whereas the task of religion is *prescriptive*, dealing with questions of value, purpose, destiny, and ultimate origin; in other words, answering "who," "why," and "what ought to be" questions.

---

19. Whitehead, *Science and the Modern World*, 181–82.
20. Haught, *God After Darwin*, 24.

Because it keeps distinctions clean, the separatist approach appeals to theologians and scientists alike. On the surface, at least, it allows the substance of theism to remain untouched by evolution, while at the same time it forbids religion and theology to intrude into the business of science. The distinction, however, appears shallow. Can religious thought remain utterly unaffected by evolution? Do not the randomness, struggle, and impersonality of the evolutionary process decisively refute theism, as the scientific skeptics have argued? Can we separate our theological convictions from what seem to be the spiritually devastating implications of evolutionary science?[21]

3. If science and religion were totally independent, the possibility of conflict would be avoided, but the possibility of constructive dialogue and mutual enrichment would also be ruled out. Life, on the whole, cannot be so neatly divided into separate compartments, since it is experienced in wholeness and interconnectedness. In the end, any adequate treatment of science and religion requires that, without giving in to temptations to conflate them anew, as occurred in the West during premodern times, we focus on ways in which they concretely affect each other.

This third, more harmonious option, views science and religion as interdependent; both are needed, and both are here to stay. The Engagement option builds on commonalities between science and religion, understanding that science needs to harness the faith, passion, and commitment of religion and that religion must learn to embrace the contributions of science and consider Darwin's "idea" not so much a danger as a great gift. Evolution, according to this third approach, can awaken in theology a fresh way of thinking about the central claims of traditional theistic faith.

Cosmic Promise Rather Than Cosmic Design

Before Darwin, many religious thinkers had argued that laws and patterns in nature could not have come about by chance, but only by intelligent design. And, of course, the intelligent designer had to be "God." Darwin, however, gave us a drastically different explanation of the design in living beings. He did not deny that nature is intricately ordered, but his theory implied that the complex patterning in living beings is the natural product of an enormously lengthy process of trial, error, and adaptation. During the course of evolution, because most organisms had been too crudely

21. Ibid., 28.

"designed" to survive in their habitats, they died out, leaving no offspring. Only relatively few, the best adapted, were able to survive and reproduce. However, if we look closely even at the survivors we can see that none of them, including ourselves, can be said to be "perfectly" designed either. Evolutionary biology calls our attention to the ample evidence of imperfect adaptation, and to the clumsy and even "wasteful" history of experiments that lies buried beneath the surface of extant life forms.

At its own level of understanding—one that refuses to engage in any theological inquiry—science has a very good explanation of design. However, evolutionary biology, like any other branch of science, is compelled to look for a purely natural explanation of design. I believe we must allow science to go as far as possible in explaining adaptive design in a "naturalistic" way, but I also affirm that evolutionary biology is only one level of a whole hierarchy of explanations needed to understand in depth the story of life. Theology can be part of such a hierarchy of explanations. Indeed I think we must at some point appeal to theology to explain ultimately why there is any order or design in nature at all—as well as why there is also instability and process. We can explain life and its complex designs on many levels without opposing one level to the other. Physics can explain order and design quite adequately from a thermodynamic point of view without interfering with biological accounts. Chemistry too can explain life at its own level. And so can theology. Problems arise only when experts on one level claim that theirs is the sole adequate explanation of life.

Darwin, along with many of his followers, concluded that the theory of evolution undermines the time-honored belief that the order or "design" in living organisms requires a divine designer. Therefore, if God is thought of primarily as an intelligent designer, evolution does appear to challenge religious belief. However, if God is thought of not simply as the ultimate source of order (or design), but also as the source of novelty (as the biblical God "who makes all things new"), then evolution is consonant with biblical faith in the God of new creation.

If we are going to speak honestly and intelligently about God after Darwin, we must do much better than simply polishing up old design arguments. There must be a better way to account for living complexity than either a pure naturalism that rejects the notion of God altogether, or a supernaturalism that must occasionally and arbitrarily appeal to the miraculous.

John Haught offers a wonderful solution.[22] He starts with the Augustinian suggestion that a creator has richly endowed the universe, from its opening moments, with the potential for evolving toward the kind of complexity we see in the cell and genetic DNA. Having done so, there is no need for God to tinker with the cosmic process. The universe is given an internal capacity for self-organization that removes the need for special divine manipulation. The sprouting of life and mind in the universe is analogous to the blossoming of an oak tree from the inauspicious beginnings of a simple acorn.

From that starting premise, Haught moves to a second possibility, that God "seeds" the universe not with design but with the promise of novelty and a complexity that eventually becomes alive and conscious, at least here on earth, but quite possibly elsewhere in the universe as well. The "word of God," which according to Genesis hovers over creation in the beginning, is a word of promise. The self-organizing universe, inseparable from God's promise of a future, may be seen as continuously moving through a "field of promise," consisting of all the possibilities offered at the start. For Haught, in some sense God (or "the Spirit of God") is this field of promise.

Haught's thesis is that cosmic purpose lies deeper than either Darwin or design. The idea of "design" is too brittle to represent the richness, subtlety, and depth of the life-process and its raw openness to the future. Life is more than "order." Life requires the continual admittance of disruptive "novelty," and so the idea of "promise" serves more suitably than "design" to indicate life's and the universe's inherent meaning. This way of "reading" evolution seems consistent both with science but also with religious hope.

The key point is that evolutionary biology, now supported and widened by cosmology, has made us realize that we live in an unfinished universe. Scientific and religious systems, together with living species and all of the cosmos, are part of a process still coming into being. The history of religion, like that of science, is a long series of partially successful but mostly inadequate human attempts to adapt to the inexhaustible depths of the cosmos (which, in part, we label "God"). Religion tries to adapt humans to the world's depth through various symbols, myths, and creeds. However, the infinite elusiveness of this depth forever evades exhaustive depiction. Hence, the religious quest, like that of science, is always frustratingly incomplete. Thus we humans, much more than animals and plants, often feel a sharp sense of dislocation and lack of correspondence to our world

22. Ibid., 92–93.

because we are made to adapt not just to actuality, but even more to possibility (what we are calling "promise"). We are, in other words, "genetically wired for a world forever open to the future."[23] The fact that the universe is even now perhaps in the early phases of its full emergence helps us understand why, religiously speaking, we remain always somewhat in the dark; why our answers to the biggest of our questions will always be frustratingly opaque; why we must walk by faith as well as by sight; and also why it makes more sense to hope than to yield to despair. The physical universe is a work in progress, and religions, firmly embedded within nature itself, are continuous with this evolutionary responsiveness. This process of adaptation can by definition never reach a static point of completion. Hence, the enormous amount of time involved in cosmic, biological, cultural, and religious evolution should come as no surprise, theologically speaking. Theology after Darwin can now suggest that the universe, understood as an adaptive process, evolves at all only because in the remote reaches of its endless depth there beckons something like a promise (this is akin to what theologians call "providence"). Promise (providence) is not manipulation of nature, but is instead a reservoir of possibilities offered to the world throughout its creative spread.

Living in a post-Darwinian universe, where evolution is a fact of life, does not demand that we give up the idea of God. Rather it asks that we think about God in a fresh way. Evolutionary knowledge, accepted and rightly viewed, can help blunt centuries of world-fleeing mystical spirituality and align our religious existence with the natural zest for life that links us biologically to our evolutionary past. The inherent adventurousness of religion may then receive a new birth. For a growing number of Christians today, evolution is a helpful and even a necessary ingredient in our thinking about God today. As the Roman Catholic theologian Hans Küng put it, evolutionary theory makes possible (1) a deeper understanding of God—not above or outside the world but in the midst of evolution; (2) a deeper understanding of creation—not as contrary to but as making evolution possible; and (3) a deeper understanding of humans as organically related to the entire cosmos.[24]

Skeptics, of course, will immediately ask how we can reconcile our ideas about a providential God with the role that chance plays in life's

---

23. Haught, *Deeper Than Darwin*, 145.
24. Küng, *Does God Exist?*, 347.

evolution.[25] This is a crucial question, which the Separation camp cannot address with finality, since it questions the reality of chance, attributing it to human ignorance of some larger divine plan. The Engagement model, however, acknowledges chance to be quite real, but does not find that it contradicts the idea of God. On the contrary, if there exists a loving God who is intimately related to the world, we should expect an aspect of indeterminacy or randomness in nature. The reason is simple: love typically operates not in a coercive but in a persuasive manner. It refuses to force itself upon the beloved, but instead allows the beloved—in this case the entire created cosmos—to remain itself, though in such a way as to imply intimacy rather than abandonment.

If, as our religious traditions have always insisted, God truly cares for the well-being of the world, then the world must be permitted to be something other than God. Even if it derives its being fundamentally from God, it must have a certain amount of "freedom" or autonomy. If the world did not somehow exist on its own, it would be nothing more than an extension of God's own being, and hence not be a world unto itself. If the world is to be anything distinct from God, it has to have room for experimenting with different ways of existing. Leaving room for such latitude does not mean that there is no divine vigilance, but only that out of respect for the otherness of creation, divine love does not crudely intrude. God risks allowing the cosmos to exist in relative liberty, and in the story of life, the world's inherent "freedom" manifests itself through the random variations or genetic mutations that comprise the raw material of evolution. A certain amount of chance is consonant with a panentheistic understanding of God.

If God were a magician or a dictator, then we might expect the universe to be finished all at once and to remain eternally unchanged. But what an impoverished world that would be; it would lack all the drama, diversity, adventure, and intense beauty that evolution has in fact produced. A world of human design might have a listless harmony to it, and it might be a world devoid of pain and struggle, but it would have none of the novelty, contrast, danger, upheaval, and grandeur provided by evolution over billions of years.

Fortunately, the God of our perspective is not a magician but a creator. And this God is more interested in promoting freedom and the adventure of evolution than in preserving the status quo. The long creative struggle of

---

25. The material in the remainder of this segment is adapted from Haught, *Science and Religion*, 61–63.

the universe to arrive at life, consciousness, and culture is consonant with the conviction that real love never forces a particular outcome but always allows for freedom, risk, adventure—and also suffering—on the part of the beloved.

Viewed in this light, the evolution of the cosmos is more than just compatible with faith in a God of self-giving love; it actually anticipates an evolving universe. It would be very difficult for us to reconcile the religious teaching about God's infinite self-giving love with any other kind of cosmos.

Levels of Reality

In his 1976 book, *Forgotten Truth*, the renowned scholar of comparative religions, Huston Smith, delves into the "primordial tradition," the common, fundamental experience of humankind, as found in the core teachings of the world's religions, identifying therein a cosmology based on the idea of an ontological gradation of reality.

According to Smith, the "primordial tradition" is perhaps best distinguished by its recognition of the many-layered nature of both reality and the self. Smith narrows these layers to four: reality is composed of the terrestrial, intermediate, celestial, and infinite levels, while the self is composed of the body, mind, soul, and spirit.

These tiers correlate in such a way that higher levels of reality correspond to deeper levels of the self:

- The terrestrial tier (also called the material, physical, sensible, corporeal, and phenomenal) corresponds to the body.

- The intermediate tier (also called the subtle, psychic, or astral) corresponds to the mind.

- The celestial tier (this realm views God as personal; here one speaks of God's attributes and personality) corresponds to the soul.

- The Infinite tier (this realm views God as transpersonal; this level is best spoken of through analogy, in negative terms, or through paradox) corresponds to the Spirit.

Smith's cosmological image shows the earth, symbolic of the terrestrial sphere, enveloped by the intermediate sphere, which in turn is enclosed by the celestial, the three concentric spheres together superimposed on a background that represents the Infinite. "Considered in itself, each sphere appears as a complete and homogeneous whole, while from the perspective of the area that encloses and permeates it, it is but a content. Thus the terrestrial world knows not the intermediate world, or the latter the celestial, though each world is known and dominated by the one that exceeds and enfolds it."[26] With each higher level, different laws apply, together with a different way of experiencing reality. The highest and deepest tiers, Infinite and Spirit, are, according to Smith, without limitation; while the Infinite is unbounded externally, the human Spirit is unbounded internally. These two levels, therefore, are in fact the same.

As one moves down the tiers of reality and out the tiers of selfhood, one encounters increasing levels of differentiation and/or materialization. In the primordial tradition, the possibility exists that one of the higher metaphysical levels can "break through" into one of the lower levels, in so doing overriding the laws of that lower level. While religion explores all four levels holistically, the laws of science are limited in their application primarily to the physical (terrestrial) level.

Going Deeper: Reflection for Participants

1. Since the doctrines of God and creation appear linked, both biblically and theologically, how might changes in our understanding of God impact our understanding of the doctrine of creation?

2. Does the biblical doctrine of creation focus primarily on origins (of the cosmos and of humans) or relationships (between humans and God, others, and themselves), and thereby with human meaning and purpose in the universe?

3. How would you respond to a person who argues that the accounts found in Genesis 1–11 are mythological?

4. Evaluate the merits of the author's statement that the original setting of Genesis 1–3 "is not a laboratory or a classroom but rather corporate worship."

5. What does this chapter say about stewardship?

6. Assess the merit of Augustine's "principle of accommodation" for reading and interpreting scripture.

26. Smith, *Forgotten Truth*, 61.

7. In your estimation, is it possible to be both "a creationist *and* an evolutionist," as Dobzhansky argued? If so, explain how such a synthesis might be constructed.

8. If the notion of evolution is determined to be compatible with Christian teaching, what is it about Darwin's version of evolution that has been so disturbing? Can Darwin's theory of evolution actually enhance one's understanding of God? Explain your answer.

9. Assess the merits of the Engagement position regarding science and religion? Are you optimistic that greater numbers of traditional Christians might commit to this perspective? What problems remain to be worked out?

10. Do you find John Haught's notion of "promise" in the universe attractive? Why or why not?

11. Assess the usefulness of Huston Smith's cosmological and anthropological correlation.

12. In your estimation, what is the primary insight gained from this session?

Session 8

Rethinking Evil, Sin, Death, and Hell
Natural or Supernatural?

Getting Started

Homework Assignment: Answer the following questions, writing your answer in your journal. Be prepared to share your views with others in the class. 1. Is evil situational, systemic, cosmic supernatural, or somehow all of the above? Support your answer. 2. Are sickness, disaster, and death natural occurrences, divine forewarnings of eternal retribution for sin and disobedience, or somehow both? 3 Is hell temporal and existential, eternal and permanent, or somehow both? Support your answer.

Gaining Momentum

As we know, starting theological discussions with the Spirit model rather than the monarchical model of God affects the meaning of a number of central Christian teachings. It does so by changing the framework in which things are seen. In this session we will explore how the Spirit model transforms our understanding of sin and the human condition.

Our central problem is not sin and guilt, as it is within the monarchical model, but "estrangement," meaning that humans are separated from that to which they belong. Our problem is blindness to the presence of God, separation from the Spirit that is all around us and within us and to which we belong. For the monarchical model, sin is primarily disloyalty to the king, seen especially as disobedience to his laws. The Spirit model addresses "sin" in more profound ways: for the metaphor of God as lover, sin is unfaithfulness; for the metaphor of God as the compassionate one who cares for all her children, sin is failure in compassion. Thus sin remains, but as betrayal of relationship and absence of compassion. Repentance also remains, only now it does not require sacrifice and contrition but a turning and returning to that to which we belong. Judgment also remains, only now not as the threat of eternal judgment but rather as living with the consequences of our choices. To remain estranged from God is to remain unsatisfied and unfulfilled.

Up to this point, attention for each session has been on one topic, an approach daunting in itself. Now you are being asked to juggle four topics at once, a seemingly impossible task. While an entire chapter could be devoted to each, I expect that participants in this study, having progressed thus far, have reached a deep level of insight and ability. This book, together with previous studies, is creating new brain cells and new neural pathways, expanding intuition and insight. These resources will enable you to progress more rapidly than before, allowing you to discern how theological topics interrelate, particularly when viewed through the prism of a specific topic, in this case the concept of evil. This session explore the nature, origin, and effects of evil. We will not sugarcoat evil, nor will we be sidetracked by easy solutions or needless superstition.

Three Kinds of Evil

When we examine actual evil around us, we detect three kinds: moral evil, pain, and natural evil. *Moral evil* is found only in human life and society because only humans are capable of moral choices. While Christian teaching makes humans wholly accountable for moral evil, we need to avoid two possible misunderstandings. On the one hand, Christianity does not teach that single persons are responsible for all the evil in their lives and for nothing else. None of us lives in isolation. We are all bound together and interrelated on numerous levels. Whatever we do, whether for good or evil, influences the people around us and those who will come after us, much as we are influenced by our neighbors and those who came before us.

On the other hand, we must not so exaggerate the social solidarity that we place the entire responsibility for the evil in our world upon our ancestors. Ezekiel dealt with people who blamed their ancestors for the political disaster that had overtaken Jerusalem, insisting that they should bear their own share of the blame: "What do you mean by repeating this proverb concerning the land of Israel, 'The parents have eaten sour grapes, and the children's teeth are set on edge'? As I live, says the Lord God, this proverb shall no more be used by you in Israel . . . ; it is only the person who sins that shall die" (Ezek. 18:2–4).

This attitude of irresponsibility is carried to an extreme if we say that all the evil in human life is due to the sin of our first ancestor, Adam. The story of Genesis 3 was not intended to be read as history. A study of Hebrew names in Genesis 3 indicates that we are dealing here with myth—a story that is true of any person at any period of history. The story of Adam is the story of every person—your story and mine. It is true that in the history of Christian thought the story of the Garden of Eden has often been misinterpreted to mean that all human beings are sinners because they inherit the taint of Adam and Eve's "original sin." But that idea is now wholly discredited, and if Christians use the phrase "original sin" today, they mean by it that we are all affected by the sinister accumulation of wrong.

There are then two kinds of moral evil: the weakness of human nature, for which we are not personally responsible, though we suffer from it daily; and the actual wrong choices we make when we had the opportunity to choose otherwise.

The *problem of pain* is more complicated, a subject we dare approach only with hesitation. It is easy to say that suffering is a discipline that ennobles the character, but not so easy to endure that discipline when we experience it directly. We can however call attention to three facts that will make plain the real problem. First, the capacity to feel pain is one of our most valuable forms of self-protection. It is a warning of danger from without and of disease from within. Secondly, while humans cannot be held responsible for disease germs, a vast amount of the suffering and sorrow cause by disease would be eliminated if it were not for human ignorance, folly, and vice. Thirdly, in a world where people break moral laws, it is better that they should suffer directly for their own sin. Laws that may be broken with impunity are not laws but chaos.

The real problem is not the existence of pain but its distribution, for its impact seems disproportionate to human character and behavior. Questions regarding the fairness of life and the justice of God surface whenever tragedy strikes, in every age and place across the globe. If everyone suffered exactly in proportion to his or her deserts, our sense of justice would be satisfied. However, as long as we think of pain in terms of justice, it will remain a mystery. Justice is not the final truth of the universe. Most of us receive more benefits that we deserve, sharing one another's joys and triumphs, and many of our sins go unpunished.

When it comes to suffering and pain, most important is not what happens to us but how we respond. Though not always welcome, pain has proven to be a great mentor, valuable for its transformative potential. The following list represents some reasons I am grateful for pain, whether physical, emotional, and spiritual:

1. Pain creates perspective.
2. Pain builds character.
3. Pain produces compassion.
4. Pain instills hope.
5. Pain enhances listening skills.
6. Pain increases self-awareness.
7. Pain brings us closer to God.
8. Pain makes us appreciate better times.
9. Pain makes us feel alive.
10. Pain lets us know things could be worse.

Natural evil includes such things as earthquakes, tidal waves, and hurricanes. A great deal of distress is caused by natural disasters of this kind, but it is nevertheless doubtful whether we ought to call them evil. Would a world without such calamities really be better than the world we know? In order to answer this question we must ask: Better for what? If you think that the purpose of life is comfort and security, then an earthquake must be considered an evil. If you think that the purpose of life is the training of character, then surely it is well that humans should live in a world that presents opportunities for heroism and vitality. That people die suddenly and in large numbers is a tragedy, but such catastrophes should not obscure our judgment. For we must all die sooner or later, and while dying today in one's forties is a calamity, to have done so in earlier centuries meant one had lived a long life.

The reality of death, which Paul called our "last enemy" (1 Cor. 15:26), can be seen to be a necessary part of the economy of nature. In the animal kingdom, the rate of reproduction is such that without death the sea would rapidly become a solid mass of fish. The human birth rate is high enough to put a serious strain on the world's food supply without the complication of having people live for ever. How intolerable would life on earth be if it were endless? The Christian explanation of this contradiction is that death is meant to be the gateway from life to life eternal, the way by which humans, having here accomplished their initial training, might pass to a fuller life in the presence of God. To those who live without God and without hope in this world, death is the blotting out of a creature with eternity in his or her nature.

The Problem of Evil

A major concern for humans, no matter their race, background, or creed, is the problem of evil. The reality of evil, whether natural (in the realm of nature) or anthropological (in the human realm), has been particularly problematic for monotheists, who must reconcile the presence of evil (including suffering and death) with belief in the goodness of the God who created the world.

In antiquity, the simplest religious explanation was to attribute evil to the actions of the gods. They seemed capricious, and if humans were to survive, they needed to appease the deities. Eventually, more complex answers arose. Some treated evil as illusory; others envisioned it as cosmic, attributing equal status to evil and good. Some acknowledged its presence within the rhythm of nature and simply learned to cope, while others limited it to human decision-making and behavior. Whatever its nature, evil affects humans where they live and must be understood on that level.

Evil is real, particularly for those who believe in God. When theists examine their world, disfigured with cruelty, disease, vice, and injustice, the reality of evil initially provides them with a conundrum, forcing them to choose between the power and the goodness of God. Either God detests evil but cannot do anything about it, in which case God is good but not almighty, or else God could put a stop to evil but wills not to, in which case God is almighty but not good. Taking seriously the reality of cosmic evil and human suffering, theologians have constructed elaborate intellectual arguments (known as theodicies) to defend God's existence or goodness.

Modern unbelievers, examining the same world, declare evil's presence temporary, an aberration to be eliminated through progress, whether cultural, scientific, educational, or technological.

The problem of evil arises for the believer out of the meeting of three beliefs: that God is good, that God is almighty, and that evil is real. We may avoid the dilemma of the Christian by denying any one of these propositions. For example, a denial of the omnipotence of God leads to dualism, the belief that the good principle behind the universe is eternally at war with an independent principle of evil. This belief was devised to explain the origin of evil, and initially it might seem to be a most satisfactory explanation. However, this explanation is profoundly inadequate. For if evil is one of the two ultimate realities of the universe, then it is as natural as good it has as much right to be there as good has. However, as soon as we regard evil as natural, we cannot consider it as an intruder in the universe that ought not to be there at all.

If, on the other hand, we deny the goodness of God, we lapse into pantheism, which says that everything that exists is a manifestation of God, and that things seem to be evil only because we see them from the wrong point of view. If we could only take God's view of the world, we would see that all things fit into a perfect pattern. However, if one believes that from the point of eternity murder, rape, fraud, and treason are but facsimiles of fidelity, chastity, honesty, and heroism, one has denied that evil is really evil.

All attempts to escape from the theistic dilemma, therefore, end in a denial of the reality of evil. The theist has the difficult task of accounting for evil, but other people have the much harder task of explaining away the evil that we all know to be real. I do not intend here to prove that evil is real, however. Such a proof might be considered necessary by those to whom evil is an intellectual problem to be solved, but not by those to whom evil is an enemy to be defeated.

Intellectual theories of evil may be grouped into two classes, depending on whether they consider evil to be a temporary imperfection or a permanent element in the makeup of the world. The imperfection theories declare that evil is a necessary step in the progress of the world toward its ultimate goal, a sort of universal growing pains. Human wrongdoing, for example, is necessary for the development of one's character. But if evil is a kind of sowing of some wild oats in the harvest of virtue, if what we call evil is an indispensable condition of virtue, then it is not really evil at all. If human sin is the path to sanctity, then Adam fell upwards. While such behavior may be a byproduct of life, we need not condone it. In intellectual theories of the second type, evil is sometimes compared to discord in music, which serves to enhance the beauty of the composition that follows. Such a view has value, for it sets off the good and increases its appreciation. However, a result does not necessarily indicate a purpose. The person who misses a flight and thus escapes a plane accident did not miss the flight intentionally. Evil may have a good or redemptive end, but if we say that evil exists in order to enhance that which is good, then it is not evil at all. Discord is not necessarily wrong; in its proper place, it has value.

The problem of dealing with evil theoretically is that if we find a reason for its existence, it ceases to be evil. The only safe way to deal with evil is not to explain it but to defeat it.

The Source of Evil

When humans explore the origin of evil in the world, questions abound. Is evil eternal? If not, did the world go wrong of its own accord? If so, was it wholly good in the first place? Those options don't appeal to theists. But if God made the world good, and it has become perverted, how did this happen? Christian theology lays the blame at the door of Satan or humanity. In each case, evil has its source in an act of free choice. Evil came into the world because either Satan or humans chose to disobey God. It is unproductive to try to trace the origin of evil back a step by asking why this choice was wrong rather than right. For a free choice is free precisely because it has no cause outside itself. It is the genius of theism that it shows how evil could have entered the world without explaining why.

Freedom is the ability to do either right or wrong; a creature that could do no wrong would be equally incapable of doing right. According to Christian theology, the possibility of evil is the risk that God took in making creatures that could relate to other creatures morally and lovingly. God was under no compulsion to create the world and the potential for human life, but God chose to create creatures that could relate intelligently and freely. With freedom came moral responsibility. Humans could not do right unless it were possible for them to do wrong.

One of the most attractive and persuasive Christian theodicies was devised in North Africa by medieval theologian Augustine, bishop of Hippo. By the fourth century, the problems raised by the existence of evil and suffering had become a theological embarrassment to Christians living in a pagan world. Manichaeism, a form of Gnosticism that fascinated Augustine as a young adult, had no difficulty in accounting for the existence of evil. Viewing the cosmos as essentially evil, the Manicheans explained its origin in the fundamentally evil nature of matter. The entire purpose of salvation was to redeem humanity from the evil material world, and transfer it to a spiritual realm that was uncontaminated by matter.

Augustine could not accept this explanation. It might offer a convenient solution to the problem of evil, yet it was incompatible with the biblical worldview. For Augustine, creation and redemption were the work of the same God. It was therefore impossible to ascribe the existence of evil to creation, for this merely transferred blame to God. For Augustine, God created the world good, meaning that it was free from the contamination of evil. So where did evil originate? Augustine's fundamental insight was that evil is a direct consequence of the misuse of human freedom. God created humanity with the freedom to choose good or evil. Sadly, humanity chose evil. As a result, the world is contaminated by evil.

Augustine's solution, known as the doctrine of privation, explains evil as human rebellion, as a turning away from God. As in the world of physics, where cold is defined as "the absence of heat," so in the world of theology, evil is defined as "the absence of good." Avoiding the trap of dualism, which views evil as eternal or matter as evil, Augustine argued that evil originated in human disobedience, in an act of the will. Evil arose historically as something good gone bad.

As Augustine himself realized, however, this explanation did not fully resolve the problem. For how could humans choose evil if there was no evil to choose? Evil had to be an option within the world if it were to be accessible to human choice. Augustine therefore located the origin of evil in satanic temptation, by which Satan lured Adam and Eve away from obedience to their creator. In this way, he argued, God could not be regarded as being responsible for evil. This explanation, however, still did not resolve the problem. For where did Satan come from if God created the world good? Augustine traced the origin of evil back another step, arguing that Satan, originally created good, is a fallen angel, who rebelled against God and thus spread that rebellion to the world. But how, Augustine's critics asked, could a good angel turn out to be so bad? How are we to account for Satan's original fall? The problem had simply been pushed back a step.

Augustine's explanation, though not fully adequate, continues to persuade. Evil is real, but it exists only through the perversion of that which was created good. Evil derives not only its existence but also its power from the good that it distorts. A small evil results from the corruption of a small good, and a great evil results from the corruption of a great good. If a person of weak intellect and reduced ability goes wrong, he can be a petty nuisance to society, but he cannot be a master criminal. But when a person of fine intellect and great ability goes wrong, he can affect the course of world history. Furthermore, we understand evil only by contrasting it with the good that it perverts. We recognize disease as an evil by contrasting it with health, and vice by contrasting it with virtue. One who cheats is a bad person because he ought to play fair. A mass murderer violates the moral law found in nature, which compels humans to preserve life, because he ought to treat others with dignity and compassion. In that single word "ought" is the justification for the whole Christian approach to evil.

We can now see more clearly the fundamental weakness of dualism as an answer to the problem of evil. For dualism attempts to make evil independent of goodness. But an eternal power of evil is unthinkable, for evil is essentially destructive, and utter evil would be utter destruction. Evil is a parasite that lives only by preying upon the good.

Original Sin: Theology Meets Biology

Sin, traditionally understood, is the problem from which we need deliverance. It is commonly understood as the reason for Jesus' death: he died for our sins (Rom. 3:23–25; 5:6–8). Indeed, in many forms of Christianity, we could not be forgiven if it were not for Jesus' sacrifice on the cross. Sin is thus the reason for the incarnation. If we had not sinned, Jesus' life and death would not have been necessary. Thus for centuries, Christians have seen the central issue separating humans from God as "sin." This doctrine, traditionally understood, has come to be called "original sin."

Some attribute the doctrine to Paul, but that is not correct. While Paul maintains that sin entered the world through Adam (Rom. 5:12), he never uses the wording "original sin," and he does not speak of a fall from previous grace. However, it was while reflecting on Romans 5:12 that in the fourth century Augustine developed the doctrine of original sin. Augustine's discussion belongs to the realm of systematic theology, while Paul's discussion resorts to typology, comparing Adam as a type to Jesus the antitype (see Rom. 5:14–21, especially v. 14). What dominates Paul's picture of Adam is his theology of Jesus. In other words, Paul did not read Genesis and come to understand Jesus; rather he understood Jesus and then read Genesis in that light. This retrospective approach means that Paul really has nothing novel to teach us about the historical origins of the human race. Paul's primary interest is not in the sin of Adam but in the grace of Christ. He contends that Christ's act of righteousness led to justification and life for all. Rather than teach universal sinfulness, some use this passage to argue for universal salvation.

The classic doctrine of original sin has two separable parts. One is the historical claim that the first human beings, Adam and Eve, sinned by eating fruit forbidden them by God. The second is the psychological claim that human nature was once virtuous, but was corrupted by the first sin. Both claims, however, can be shown to be false. As Patricia Williams demonstrates in her groundbreaking book *Doing without Adam and Eve*, the alleged corruption of human nature is found neither in Genesis 3 nor anywhere else in the Hebrew scriptures. Genesis 3:22 explicitly states that Adam and Eve became more like gods after they ate the fruit of the tree of knowledge. The idea of a fall—a corruption in human nature—is also not prominent in the New Testament; the event of Genesis 3 is only mentioned in two passages, both Pauline (Rom. 5:12–21, 1 Cor. 15:21–22). Only later, in the writings of Augustine, did the doctrine of original sin become formulated in any significant way.

In the past, religion and philosophy provided humans with explanations and definitions of good and evil. Nowadays, however, modern people are increasingly looking to science for the kind of updated information they need to cope with evils such as birth defects, natural disasters, and disease. In a chapter titled "The Demise of Adam and Eve," Williams asserts that it took the birth of modern science to challenge the predominant model of the universe and of human nature that had survived for over a thousand years. The scientific theory of biological evolution made clear that successful species like humans do not pass through single-pair bottlenecks; there is certainly no evidence that this was true of *Homo sapiens*, a species that seems to have been well spread around the earth. Genetic evidence indicates that human populations never consisted of fewer than several thousand individuals.

Scientifically speaking, Adam and Eve can no longer be viewed as the progenitors of humanity, for they were not historical figures. If not historical figures, they could not have disobeyed God. If they did not disobey God, then we have no basis for original sin and therefore no fall and no corruption of human nature.[1] Thus, the narrative about them cannot be used to explain the human inclination to sin or the origin of evil. That said, there is no need for despair. If one is prepared to accept a metaphorical interpretation of the Adam and Eve story, while insisting on the relevance of evolution, a ready understanding of original sin emerges.

As Darwinians have demonstrated, the struggle for existence and the consequent selection of variations leading to adaptations designed for success in this struggle often involve self-interest, if not outright selfishness, with the host of features, attitudes, and characteristics that most humans find offensive and that Christians judge as sinful. Of course, to be self-interested is not necessarily to be immoral. No one judges ill the person who eats a meal because he or she is hungry, or who falls in love with a pretty girl or a handsome young man and wants to have that person as a mate. But, all too quickly, self-interest degenerates into qualities like greed, lust, and boastfulness. There are good biological reasons for this. Those who feed themselves or their families are better off than those who have no food or just leftover scraps. The man who impregnates a hundred women is ahead (in the Darwinian game of survival) of a man who impregnates just one. The person who lies and cheats his way to the top of the corporate ladder is more successful than he who loses.

Original sin as part of the biological package comes with being human. We inherit it from our parents and they from their parents. Moreover, overlapping our selfishness is a genuine altruism, a very necessary adaptation given the human path of sociality. We are loving, kind, and generous because that is just as much a part of our nature as is our selfishness. Acknowledging that sin remains central to the human condition, Williams supplies insights from the field of sociobiology, such as the influence of genes, the environment, and the misuse of human freedom, to account for the origin of sin and to deal with the problem of evil. With respect to original sin, sociobiological *Homo sapiens* are practically identical to Christian *Homo sapiens*. Both camps see humans as deeply self-centered, selfish even, but with a genuine moral overlay, guiding (at least, instructing) our actions in social situations and interactions. The surface stories are very different, but the underlying concerns are the same: humans are truly sinful, with goodness fighting for control.

As understood by Augustine, who coined the term, original sin is a biologically transmitted tendency to evil desires (*libido*) that arose with

---

1. Williams, *Doing without Adam and Eve*, xiv, 79–80.

Adam and has contaminated all of humanity. However, most theologians today would consider such an interpretation extremely shallow. According to contemporary theological interpretation, original sin refers not to a specific act committed by a parental couple in the remote past, but to the general state of our present human estrangement from God, from each other, and from the natural world. We are all born into a world that is already deeply flawed, in great measure by human greed and violence. The notion of original sin, in this sense, also reminds us of our human incapacity to save ourselves from this state of affairs.

The assumption of an original perfection of creation, as envisioned by creationism, has in fact led religious speculation to imagine that the source of the enormous evil and suffering in the world must be either an original principle of evil—an idea unacceptable to biblical theism, which views the creation as inherently good—or else some intraworldly being or event. The latter supposition has led to the demonizing of various events, persons, animals, genders, and races. Understanding evil as the result of an initial transgression has made reparation and expiation a priority for all who follow biblical religion. The vital problem, both for Christ and for us, is to find a culprit and remove its influence. The assumption of original sin opened up the possibility of interpreting suffering essentially as punishment, necessitating an ethic of retribution.

By contrast, it is enough for us simply to wonder what a salutary thing it would be if religious thought were now to take the reality of evolution with complete seriousness. Evolution means that the world is unfinished. And if unfinished, then we cannot justifiably expect perfection. There is inevitably a dark side. The notion that present evil can be attributed to a culprit that somehow spoiled the primordial creation has led to a misunderstanding of the "history of salvation" as a drama of "restoring" the original state of affairs. This emphasis has caused theologians to subordinate the expectation of the far more accurate and fulfilling understanding of the history of salvation as *transformation*—the novelty and surprise at the fulfillment of God's promises—to that of *restoration*—the recovery of a primal perfection of being. This is why evolution is potentially such good news for theology. Evolutionary cosmology invites us to complete the biblical vision of a life based on openness to the future and hope for surprise rather than allowing us to wax nostalgic for what we mistakenly imagine once was.

In an unfinished universe, we humans remain accomplices of evil, of course. But our complicity in evil may now be interpreted less in terms of a hypothesized break from primordial innocence than as our systematic refusal to participate in the ongoing creation of the world. According to this new way of thinking, sin and evil now include our resistance to the call of "being more," our deliberate turning away from participation in what is still coming into being. In an evolutionary context, "original" sin is also the aggregation in human history and culture of all effects of our habitual refusal to take our appropriate place in the ongoing creation of the universe. It is this kind of corruption—and not the defilement of an allegedly original cosmic perfection—by which each of us is "stained."

The Conquest of Evil

When we examine evil and its effects, we wonder what God is doing about the evil in the world. When it comes to moral evil, we recognize that God has granted freedom to human beings, and that humans cannot be compelled to be good without taking away their freedom. Yet we cannot rest content with a theory that leaves God's purpose thwarted and God's world defiled by sin. If there were no more to be said, we could hardly avoid the feeling that God would have done better not to have made the world at all than to have created a tragic failure.

The final answer of the Christian to the problem of evil is that God has done something, that in Christ God has defeated sin and death. The Christian gospel is that Christ has broken the hold of sin on human life and society, that he has shown how evil things may be redeemed and used for a good purpose, that he has taken the thorns of life and worn them as a crown of glory, and that he has transformed death from an enemy into a friend.

Is Hell Real?

Most cultures and religions of the world teach retribution for human sin. Retribution comes in many guises, including factors in this world such as guilt, karma, calamities, social determinism, and reincarnation, and factors such as purgation, annihilation, or banishment in the next.

Throughout Christian history, the doctrine of eternal punishment in hell has been a powerful deterrent to human misbehavior and disbelief, used by parents and by civil and religious authorities to manipulate, entice, control, and even to oppress. Fortunately, such instruments of conformity and coercion are no longer working, for Christians are increasingly questioning their value and validity.

In our time, belief in a God who is all-good, all-benevolent, and all-just is widely viewed as incompatible with the traditional doctrine of hell. Indeed, such a belief seems impossible. The contradiction of holding such views simultaneously is so great that many Christians today are moderating their understanding of hell, viewing the concept as a metaphor for the absence of God's presence rather than as a place of eternal punishment.

Some skeptics, following the Christian logic that non-believers will spend eternity in hell if they reject the message of the gospel, have proposed that it would be better if Christians would simply stop evangelizing the world, for then non-Christians would no longer find reasons to reject the message and thereby have a better chance of going to heaven. Others, underscoring the perverse logic of heaven and hell, have argued that the universal killing of children before they reached the hypothetical "age of accountability"—when the church considers them morally responsible—might be construed as merciful, for such would actually enhance their chances of eternal salvation.

The idea of hell, like belief in heaven, is a stepchild of the doctrine of the afterlife. If one can demonstrate that behind all thought, desire, and life there is only one prime force—a God who is love—then belief in the doctrine of hell is weakened and possibly eliminated.

The presence of the doctrine of hell in the Bible, like belief in the afterlife in general, is quite late. Before the sixth century BC, the Hebrews, along with the Phoenicians, Babylonians, Greeks, and Romans, did not emphasize life after death, for they had no clear belief in the existence of a soul as separate from the body. The dead, righteous and wicked together, survived as "shades" in an underworld called Sheol, similar to Hades in the Homeric poems, but they were limited to a dull, shadowy existence without clear consciousness. There was nothing desirable here; it was simply one step removed from annihilation. As anthropologists and social historians point out, the reason behind this emphasis was a concept known as "corporate personality," meaning that in the ancient world, the tribe was the basic social unit.

The Hebrews lived and thought tribally. When a single individual sinned, as in the classic case of Achan in the biblical account of the battle of Jericho (Josh. 7:11–26), the entire tribe was punished. According to the book of Exodus, the people of Egypt were afflicted with dreadful plagues on account of the hardness of heart of the Pharaoh. This belief made sense in an era when the overwhelming value and chief virtue was the survival of the tribe, not the survival of the individual. In the sixth century, around the time the Hebrews came under the influence of the Persians, biblical literature gives evidence of the rise of a concept of individualism. A current proverb: "The parents have eaten sour grapes, and the children's teeth are set on edge," quoted by Jeremiah and Ezekiel, was questioned by these prophets and by their generation. Ezekiel, as noted earlier, is quite possibly the first figure in Jewish religious history to assign reward and punishment based on a sense of individual responsibility.

For tribal people to think individualistically required a quantum leap in consciousness, and biblical history informs us that during the Intertestamental and New Testament periods, Jews and Jewish Christians continued to think corporately. One need recall the story of the blind man brought to Jesus by his disciples with the question: "Rabbi, who sinned, this man or his parents, that he was born blind?" (John 9:2). One possible answer, certainly on their minds, was that the individual's blindness had been caused by parental sin (the origin of the view is often attributed to the commandment in Exodus 20: 5, which declares that God punishes children for the iniquity of parents, "to the third and the fourth generation of those who reject me").

The first person believed to have had ideas about the soul perhaps close to modern notions was Zoroaster, a Persian who lived about 600 BC. As the founder of Zoroastrianism, he taught that humans have a body and a soul, and that the soul is associated with the faculties of reason, consciousness, conscience, and free will. Free will, according to Zoroastrianism, enables people to choose good or evil actions, for which they are morally responsible. Because of their actions, God is justified in rewarding or punishing individuals by sending them to heaven or hell. Following the Babylonian exile, the Jews had very close contact with the Persians, at which time Jews may have begun adopting beliefs similar to those of the Zoroastrians, including a final judgment and the resurrection of the dead.

The first Jewish text to suggest the possibility of an afterlife as a venue for righting earthly wrongs is the *Book of the Watchers*, as scholars call the work preserved as 1 Enoch 1–36. This work, which reached its final form by the end of the third century BC, was extremely influential in the Intertestamental period. In the last portion of this volume, the patriarch Enoch (mentioned in Genesis 5:21–24), is taken on a tour of the earth in the company of the archangels. After seeing the fiery abyss in which the watchers (the Nephilim of Genesis 6:4—angels who descended to earth to marry women) are imprisoned, Enoch comes to a mountain with four chambers. The passage suggests that the chambers house the souls of the dead, with the souls of the wicked relegated to the dark chambers while the souls of the righteous enjoy temporary blessing as they await their final disposition on the Day of Judgments. In at least one of the dark chambers the souls of the wicked are already undergoing punishment.

It is difficult to ascertain how quickly the new picture of the afterlife became widespread among Jews, but by 165 BC, during the Maccabean period of Jewish history, the idea of individual life after death based on merit appears in the apocalyptic book of Daniel. Apocalyptic thought was a form of prophecy that flourished in the Jewish literature of the postexilic period, beginning particularly with the Maccabean period. The chief examples in the Bible are the book of Daniel in the Old Testament and the book of Revelation, the closing book in the New Testament. This type of writing focuses on the last things and anticipates the imminent end of the world. Apocalypticism is a religious outlook that envisions a final conflict between God and the powers of evil, whereby enemies are defeated and punished while insiders, generally persecuted minorities, are rewarded in a new world order established by God. Apocalyptic literature, written by victims, expresses their hopes through visions with complex and sometimes gruesome symbolism. This outlook led to extreme characterizations of the afterlife as consisting of two options, heaven and hell. Heaven, of course, is for insiders, while hell is for the rest. Tragically, though it need hardly be mentioned, in the experience of many of our contemporaries, hell is real because it is here and it is now.

Is Satan Real?

To understand the meaning and presence of the figure of Satan in the New Testament and in Christian thought, we start with the Old Testament book of Job, a timeless drama about the meaning of life written during the postexilic period (between 550 and 350 BC). The story introduces a character called the *satan*, a member of the heavenly council. Earlier in the Bible the Hebrew word "*satan*" is used to represent human adversaries (1 Kgs. 11:14, 23, 25). In Job the *satan* appears as a supernatural being, not in an evil role, for his power is subject to God's will, but as an adversary. This character disappears after chapter 2, for the purpose of the book is not to teach that human suffering or evil are caused by Satan, but rather that they are in the hands of God. In the book of Job, the cause of suffering and evil are left unanswered.

During the period of the Babylonian exile (586–539 BC) and its aftermath, Jews grappled with theodicy, developing an understanding that posited a force that thwarted the divine will. That opposition, however, was believed to be short-lived, for in a climactic event in which the long-awaited Messiah would appear, opposition to the will of the sovereign Creator would be overcome. While they viewed evil as real, they expected it would soon be defeated decisively.

Early Christians inherited this perspective through their Jewish tradition, coming to see in the life and person of Jesus of Nazareth the answer to the rule of evil, personified by Satan. Christians felt they were living in an interim period, between the first coming of Jesus, whose mission inaugurated God's rule on earth, and the second coming of Jesus, whose second appearance would eliminate all traces of evil. Theirs was both a cosmic dualism (seeing evil and good as dimensions of reality, symbolized by earthly and heavenly realms) and a temporal dualism (consisting of a past age of evil and a future age of bliss).

Christian views of Satan have often been influenced by depictions in the book of Revelation. A series of visions in 12:1--14:20 form the central axis of the book and the core of its argument. This section constitutes one unit, a drama of operatic proportions in which "the characters and actions are exaggerated, larger than life. Chapters 12–13 pull away the curtain that hides the transcendent world from ordinary sight and offer a behind-the-scenes view of the powers of evil at work in the present, while chapter 14 proleptically presents a behind-the-scenes view of the victory of God in salvation and judgment."[2] This unit introduces some of the most dramatic images in the entire book. The four depictions of evil include Satan—the great dragon hurled from the sky to prowl the earth—and Satan's cronies, consisting of a seven-headed beast from the sea, a cunning beast from the land, and Babylon the harlot. A key to this segment is the announcement of the heavenly chorus in 11:18 that the time has come to destroy the destroyers of the earth. If God is the Creator and God's will for the world is life, then God must defeat those forces that threaten life.

The second half of Revelation is dominated by the struggle against these agents of evil. Following the plot, one discovers that John systematically

---

2. Boring, *Revelation*, 150.

introduces four depictions of imperial evil, only to defeat them—in reverse order. The harlot is first to be destroyed, when the seven-headed beast turns against her (17:16). Then the two beasts are defeated, when Christ overpowers them with the sword (the word) that comes from his mouth (19:19–20). Only Satan is left, temporarily banished from earth to the abyss below only to be hurled into the lake of fire (20:10). The second half of Revelation is the story of the defeat of these agents of evil.

While the author of Revelation incorporates references to a number of pagan myths, his purpose is to demonstrate that the true answer to people's problems is in Christ, not in paganism. As often happens in Revelation, what John sees he describes largely in traditional imagery, to which he gives Christian interpretation. Ultimately, his imagery is to be understood from its use in Revelation, not from its use in pagan myths. The "woman clothed with the sun," for example, is to be understood in contrast to the harlot Rome (17:1), whereas the dragon and beasts of chapter 13 are parodies of the Trinity.

Into the spectacular cosmic story of the woman's childbirth and rescue in the wilderness John inserts a second dramatic story, the defeat of Satan and his fall from heaven, along with his angels (Rev. 12:7–12). Since Revelation is an apocalypse, its imagery does not generally depict actual events. As modern Christians do not accept the biblical cosmology as factual, they need not view the world as a battle between angels, dragons, and a personified Satan. Furthermore, in apocalyptic literature events that take place in heaven often are reflective of events on earth. That is certainly true for John; in Revelation, everything he sees in heaven is the counterpart of some earthly reality. John tells this story to affirm that God and his Messiah are enthroned in heaven, meaning there is no sign of evil and rebellion there. This affirmation provides perspective and offers hope to those who live in a social wilderness and are threatened by local dragons. The cosmic war in heaven, with the defeat of the dragon and his angels by Michael and his angels, also depicts the heavenly, spiritual dimension of Jesus' victory on the cross, a victory Christians conceived of as a great spiritual battle in which Jesus attained cosmic victory over satanic evil. To see Satan as thrown down to the earth is to affirm that he no longer has access to God's throne.

Revelation 12 is not the first time Satan comes to earth. The author of Revelation assumes that Satan has been active in both heaven and earth since the beginning of time. So what happens is that when Satan is thrown down from heaven, his range of operation is severely limited (see Luke 10:18; cf. Rom. 16:19–20). He is limited to working on the earth, where Christians can resist his influence (Jas. 4:7; cf. 1 Pet. 5:8–9). This concept differs from the traditional idea that Satan was expelled from heaven at the dawn of time. That notion—which appears in some ancient Jewish sources—was derived in part from Isaiah 14:12, where a tyrant is associated with the fallen angel (Lucifer) and then thrown into Sheol (the Abyss). That passage was then connected to the story of creation from Genesis 3, where the serpent lures Adam and Eve into sin. By combining these texts, people concluded that when Satan was expelled from heaven he must have survived in the Garden of Eden, where he could tempt the first humans. This tradition, which achieved classic form in John Milton's epic work *Paradise Lost*, is mythical and not biblical.

Revelation's perspective is different, for John's viewpoint is based on passages from Job and Zechariah, where Satan surveys the earth, checking up on people. Revelation 12:9 provides a partial list of biblical names for Satan or the dragon, culminating in "deceiver of the whole world." According to Revelation, God no longer tolerates Satan's accusations, so the archangel Michael acts as the bouncer, confining him to the world below. In Jewish tradition Michael, one of the leading angels in heaven, is familiar from the book of Daniel, where he is called a "prince" and "protector" (Dan. 10:21; 12:1).

While the book of Revelation incorporates references to a number of pagan myths, its purpose is not to focus on their mythology or to argue that the myths be taken literally. Revelation is unique in appealing primarily to our imagination—not, however, a loose or reckless imagination, but a disciplined one. This book was not written to terrify people but to awaken them, to encourage them with the message that though evil is real, Jesus has already won the victory. Revelation should be read as a pastoral letter, not as a theological treatise.

According to the apocalyptic mindset, evil is so great that humans cannot eliminate it. Only God can do so. Unlike the apocalyptic tradition, which tended to view evil cosmically and demonically, the prophetic tradition spoke of good and evil largely in human terms. The New Testament builds upon both traditions, as does the book of Revelation. The call to Revelation's audience to "conquer" is fundamental to the structure and theme of the book. It demands the readers' active participation in the divine war against evil.

The Gospel of John, surprisingly similar to Revelation in many ways, says very little about Satan's role. This Gospel has little interest in the image of a cosmic figure responsible for evil. Rather the focus is on discipleship. If people act in evil and hurtful ways because they belong to the world and its values, how then can human evil be overcome? John's answer is neither apocalyptic nor cosmic but moral. Evil is defeated by the followers of Jesus, who, as disciples, are asked to walk in the light, as did Jesus, their Lord and master. In John's Gospel, this form of discipleship is described as living life abundantly (10:10). Other biblical writers agree with John's assessment: "Resist the devil," exhorts the author of the letter of James, "and he will flee from you. Draw near to God, and he will draw near to you" (Jas. 4:7–8). Through faithful lifestyles, by trusting in Jesus and building upon the foundation of faith, believers become conquerors with Christ. That is how evil is defeated, whether within or without: moment by moment, decision by decision, one step at a time.

Going Deeper: Reflection for Participants

1. Do you conceive of evil as essentially cosmic or anthropological in nature? Explain your answer.

2. How do you reconcile God's power and goodness with the reality of evil?

3. Should we be hopeful, optimistic, or pessimistic about human nature and destiny? Support your answer.

4. When it comes to personal suffering and pain, what does your response tend to be? How has pain been a mentor to you?

5. Assess Augustine's doctrine of privation. Do you find it adequate to explain the power and pervasiveness of evil? Support your answer.

6. What is meant by "original sin"? In your estimation, what are the merits of this doctrine? Are the insights of Patricia Williams helpful?

7. Given the biblical emphasis on the original goodness of the created order (see Genesis 1), is it possible for human nature to change from essentially good to essentially corrupt (fallen)? Explain your answer.

8. Traditional Christians and Muslims are taught to believe in a literal heaven and hell. What arguments support this view? What arguments

dispute this view? To what extent can we understand biblical and theological depictions of heaven and hell as symbolic of deeper realities? If so, what might these deeper realities be?

9. Discuss what you learned from this chapter about the origin and evolution of the biblical figure of Satan. How important is Satan to your understanding of evil?

10. How do you picture evil in the world? Is personifying Satan as a hideous beast helpful or evasive? Explain your answer.

11. What lessons about resisting evil can we learn from the account of Jesus' temptation (see Matthew 4:1–11)?

12. In your estimation, what is the primary insight gained from this session?

Session 9

Rethinking Salvation, Heaven, and Eternal Life
Utopian Afterlife or Present Grace?

Getting Started

Homework Assignment: Answer the following questions, writing your answers in your journal. Be prepared to share your views with others in the class. 1. Is salvation primarily temporal or eternal? 2. Is heaven/eternal life primarily temporal, eternal, or somehow both? Support your answer.

Gaining Momentum

By now we are aware that starting theological discussions with the Spirit model rather than the monarchical model of God affects the meaning of most if not all Christian teachings. It does so by changing the framework in which things are seen. In this session we will explore how the Spirit model transforms our understanding of the doctrine of salvation and the concept of eternal life.

The images of God associated with the Spirit model dramatically affect how we think of the Christian life. Rather than viewing God as a distant judge with whom we might spend eternity, if we get with the program, the Spirit emphasizes that God—the sacred—is right here. Rather than sin and guilt being the central dynamic of the Christian life, the central dynamic becomes relationship—with God, the world, and each other. The monarchical model promotes stability, security, conformity, and uniformity, while the Spirit model promotes newness, growth, change, and transformation.

The Meaning of the Cross: Five Interpretations

For Christians, the doctrine of salvation is closely related to the crucifixion of Jesus. This connection is already evident in the Gospels, which make the accounts of Jesus' passion central and paramount to the Christian story. Rich in meaning, the death of Jesus became the subject of theological reflection throughout Christian history.

For centuries, Christians have viewed the death of Jesus as salvific, as having saving significance and making our salvation possible. According to many Christians, the death of Jesus was the purpose of his life on earth and was central as well to God's purpose for history. In the familiar language of the Gospel of John: "For God so loved the world that he gave his only Son, so that everyone who believes in him may not perish but may have eternal life" (3:16). Likewise the Nicene Creed speaks of the saving significance of Jesus' death as the very reason he came: "For us and for our salvation he came down from heaven, (and) for our sake he was crucified under Pontius Pilate." The Gospels portray the death of Jesus as integral to his vocation, as necessary, and as the fulfillment of prophecy. Mark's Gospel, the earliest gospel, contains a threefold prediction of the passion, indicating that Jesus both taught his disciples of his imminent death and of the ensuing resurrection: "Then he began to teach them that the Son of Man must undergo great suffering, and be rejected by the elders, the chief priests, and the scribes, and be killed, and after three days rise again" (8:31; see also 9:31 and 10:32–33).

For those who read these passages as literal quotations of Jesus, the interpretation seems obvious: Jesus knew in advance the details of his death and saw them as central to his messianic vocation and purpose in life. Mainstream biblical scholarship views such prediction as post-Easter creations, for in the decades following Good Friday and Easter, the early Christian movement preserved the memory of those events by adding to their meaning. Several interpretations of the meaning of the crucifixion are found in the New Testament itself, comprising what is called "atonement theology." In the judgment of many scholars, atonement theology does not go back to Jesus himself. His crucifixion was the consequence of his actions and teaching, but not their purpose. Comparing his death with those of Mahatma Gandhi and Martin Luther King Jr., one can appreciate more clearly that these deaths were the consequence of their actions and teachings, but certainly not their intention. Looking back on the crucifixion of Jesus, the early Christian movement sought a providential purpose in this horrific event. At least five interpretations of the cross are found in the New Testament itself:[1]

1. A *political meaning*: Jesus was a threat to the Roman authorities, who executed him. The authorities said "no" to Jesus, but God has said "yes" (Acts 2:36).

2. A *cosmic meaning*: temporal rulers, whether Roman rulers or Jewish aristocrats in Judea, are viewed as subject to cosmic "principalities and powers," evil systems of domination built into human institutions. According to language found primarily in letters attributed to Paul (Col. 2:15), Jesus' death defeats such cosmic powers.

3. A *psychological meaning*: the death and resurrection of Jesus are seen as the embodiment of the path of spiritual transformation that lies at the center of the Christian life, the path of dying to an old way of being and being raised into a new way of being (Gal. 2:19–20).

4. A *spiritual meaning*: the death of Jesus reveals the depth of God's love for us (John 3:16; Rom. 5:8).

5. A *sacrificial meaning*: this view emphasizes that "Christ died for our sins" (1 Cor. 15:3). This familiar theological understanding of the cross was formulated in the Middle Ages by Anselm of Canterbury (1033–1109), who defined the doctrine of atonement that became normative in the West: God became man in order to expiate the sin of Adam.

Biblical scholar Marcus Borg argues that in its first-century setting, the statement that "Jesus is the sacrifice for sin" would not have meant that Jesus' death was part of God's plan for salvation. Rather, it would have been understood as a challenge to the sacrificial system centered in the temple in Jerusalem. According to temple theology, "certain kinds of sins and impurities could be dealt with only through sacrifice in the temple. Temple theology thus claimed an institutional monopoly on the forgiveness of sins;

---

1. Borg, *Heart of Christianity*, 91–95.

and because the forgiveness of sins was a prerequisite for entry into the presence of God, temple theology also claimed an institutional monopoly on access to God."[2] Jewish Christians, using the metaphor of sacrifice, were affirming that forgiveness is not rooted in institutional monopoly but in gracious freedom. It is ironic to realize that the Christian religion began to claim for itself a monopoly on grace and access to God that is undermined by this contextual understanding of the meaning of the cross.

The Doctrine of Salvation: From What are We Saved?

Many Christians have been reared with the sin and salvation paradigm, a view prominently upheld in evangelical preaching and teaching.[3] This view compresses the overarching storyline of the Bible into a conversionist template. It begins with absolute perfection in the Garden of Eden, followed by a Fall into original sin (it is important to note that terms such as "Fall" and "original sin," while essential to this paradigm, are not found in the Bible). As a consequence of the sin of Adam and Eve, all humans find themselves in a state of condemnation. Unable to save themselves (that is, to be restored to proper relationship with God, others, themselves, and nature), they are dependent upon God's grace to provide a way of redemption. Because of God's great love for humanity, God sent Jesus to die in our place. God's gift, however, must be accepted by faith, and those who accept Christ as Savior are assured of eternity in heaven with God. Those who remain unrepentant or in a fallen state—which represents the vast majority of humans according to some versions of this conventional view— face damnation to hell, defined traditionally as banishment from God and eternal torment.

Traditional Christians sometimes modify this story line, but rarely do they question its trajectory as a whole, its morality, or even whether it is truly biblical. If it is biblical, did Abraham hold it, or Moses, or Isaiah, or Jesus? Is it explicitly taught in scripture? Was it held in the first three centuries of Christian history? Surprisingly, the answer to each question is "no."

While the Christian tradition tends to present the doctrine of salvation in terms of the ultimate destiny of the individual, this is not accurate, for as the etymology of the word demonstrates, "salvation" comes from the Latin words *salutas*, meaning "security, safety, or wholeness" and *salvus*,

2. Ibid., 94.
3. This segment on sin and salvation is taken from my earlier book, *Beyond Belief*, 28–29.

meaning something "whole, intact, or in good working order." In biblical times, as today, a viable religion must keep its social system intact, meaning it has to provide salvation at the social level. The majority of current Christian scholars are convinced that the modern evangelical emphasis on "being saved," which views salvation primarily as an assurance of entrance to heaven, is at best a rather recent emphasis in Christian tradition, going back no earlier than the nineteenth century.

In the Bible the concept of salvation had an essentially this-worldly orientation, meaning that the concept was used to assure believers of security from physical and external threats and to guarantee their place in the coming kingdom of God on earth. The paradigmatic model for salvation is the exodus from bondage in Egypt. The Song of Moses, a hymnic passage about the exodus, proclaims God as the "salvation" of the Israelites (Exod. 15:2; see Ps. 106:21) because God was instrumental in their deliverance from oppression. They were later saved from various other oppressors, sometimes through a human being sent for that purpose: "The Lord gave Israel a savior, so that they escaped from the hand of the Arameans" (2 Kgs. 12:5). During the Babylonian exile, God is said to have prepared Cyrus of Persia to carry divine salvation to the Israelites yet again (Isa. 44:28—45:7). Thus the prophet Jeremiah could call God the "hope of Israel, its savior in time of trouble" (Jer. 14:8).

The doctrine of salvation is complex, and different aspects of the Christian understanding of sin and salvation have been emphasized by theologians, teachers, or by different sects and denominations during different periods of church history or for specific situations. Recent studies of the biblical notion of salvation emphasize the importance of contextualization, meaning that because the Christian gospel always addresses specific situations, the doctrine of salvation should be contextualized in those circumstances. For example, to the oppressed—whether spiritually, economically, or politically—the gospel message is that of liberation; to those burdened by personal guilt, the message is one of forgiveness; to the despondent, the message is one of hope.

Christianity holds that the created order, particularly humanity, has fallen into disorder. Things are not what they were meant to be, and something needs to be done about this. The same God who made the created order must act to reorder it, something God accomplished through the life, death, and resurrection of Jesus Christ. In his widely used text *Christian Theology*, Alistair McGrath provides answers given by Christians throughout their history to the question, "*from* what are we saved?" In each case, the doctrine of sin provides an answer. Each model, in turn, also points to the doctrine of salvation, with its hopeful answers.[4]

From what, then, are we saved? McGrath provides six answers: Christians are saved from (1) their human condition, (2) their guilt, (3) their lack of holiness, (4) their inauthentic human existence (characterized by faith in the transient material world), (5) oppression, and (6) from forces that enslave humanity—such as satanic forces, evil spirits, fear of death, or the power of sin. In summary, the Christian doctrine of salvation deals with the restoration of all things, including humanity, to its proper relationship to God.

The Doctrine of Salvation: For What Are We Saved?

Salvation, consequently, represents new possibilities, a new state of being. McGrath provides models of salvation that correspond to the six models of sin. Together, they answer the question, "*for* what are we saved?" Christians are saved for (1) relationship with God, (2) righteousness in the sight of God, (3) personal holiness, (4) authentic human existence, (5) social and political liberation, and (6) spiritual freedom.

The understanding of salvation presented above exhibits a radical this-worldly orientation. The reason is clear: traditional Christians followed their Jewish counterparts in placing their faith into a historical context. The basic conviction of the Greeks was that truth was changeless and hence not tied to events. The earliest Christian creeds, such as the Apostles' Creed, were composed to counter such views, which tended to overspiritualize Jesus and detach Christianity from history.

Belief in the Afterlife

As we noted in Session 7, the habit of thinking individualistically as opposed to corporately in the Bible is rather late, as is the idea of heaven and the afterlife. The book of Daniel, composed during a precarious time in Jewish history, less than two centuries before the birth of Christianity, emphasizes God's providential role in history. Daniel is one of the few books in the Hebrew Bible that can be reliably dated. The book is said to set forth

---

4. McGrath, *Christian Theology*, 339–42.

the theology of the Maccabean revolution and to represent the manifesto of the Hasidim. The book's final form, especially the second half, can be dated to the period 167–164 BC, when the Seleucid tyrant Antiochus IV Epiphanes ruled the Jewish homeland. While the author of the book of Daniel remains unknown, he belonged to the resistance movement called the Hasidim ("faithful ones"), a group of nonconformists who resisted the Seleucid policy of Hellenization, a coercive policy that forced Jews to compromise or abandon key distinctives such as monotheism, the Sabbath, circumcision, purity codes, kosher food laws, and the sacrificial system.

In Daniel 12, those who resist the enforced Seleucid program of Hellenization are called "the wise." It is they who are promised a glorious and eternal future: "Many of those who sleep in the dust of the earth shall awake, some to everlasting life, and some to shame and everlasting contempt" (Dan. 12:2). Here, according to some scholars, we have the first explicit biblical reference to resurrection. Further confirmation of second- and first-century Jewish belief in a corporeal resurrection comes from the apocryphal book of 2 Maccabees, written in Greek in the decades following the Maccabean revolt (167–163 BC). The story of the extreme torture and martyrdom of seven brothers in chapter 7 presupposes a resurrection of the body and even a reassembling of dismembered limbs, while the passage in 12:43–44 assumes on the basis of resurrection that prayers for the dead are efficacious (see also 1 Cor. 15:29). The Maccabean material clearly grew out of the need for justice. If young Jewish people died as martyrs rather than compromise their faith, then surely God must reward them.

Earlier biblical references to the afterlife, including the notoriously difficult passage in Job 19:26–27 and the undateable Isaiah 26:19, are unclear in the original Hebrew version and cannot support the later doctrinal meaning imposed on them by Christian translators. Two passages found in the book of Ecclesiastes also should be mentioned. The remark about the possibility of an afterlife inserted in Ecclesiastes 3:21 should not be interpreted out of context, since it is prefaced by the clearer meaning of the preceding verse: "All go to one place; all are from the dust, and all turn to dust again." Another passage, Ecclesiastes 12:7, suggests that the human breath or "spirit" returns to God, but this verse is simply affirming the viewpoint of Genesis 2:7, in which human life and death are said to be dependent upon the breath of God, which returns at death to God, from whence it came.

By the start of the Christian era, Jews disagreed on eschatological beliefs, with the Sadducees holding the older belief that there is no afterlife and consequently no resurrection and the Pharisees accepting the newer belief that there is an afterlife as well as a resurrection. Belief in rewards and punishments became significant in rabbinic Judaism, which emerged in the aftermath of the destruction of the temple in AD 70. The apostle Paul, called "the second founder of Christianity" for his theological influence on earliest Christianity, was a Pharisee before his conversion. Through him, the key doctrinal beliefs of the Pharisees became central to Christianity, including their doctrine of the afterlife.

It is important to keep in mind that the New Testament remains ambiguous about life after death. While the idea of Jesus' resurrection is central to Christianity, its meaning is debated within the New Testament. As Paul writes in 1 Corinthians 15:50, "flesh and blood cannot inherit the kingdom of God, nor does the perishable inherit the imperishable." And Paul did not address the notion of hell. As scholars now note, most of the images of fire and torment in the afterlife come from the Gospel of Matthew and the book of Revelation. As notions of heaven and hell evolved over time in the Christian tradition, related concepts and adjustments were added, including such notions as purgatory, limbo, and child limbo. Since all sins were not considered equal, time sentences and other forms of plea-bargaining entered the equation.

In his *Divine Comedy*, Dante Alighieri gives poetic expression to medieval Christian beliefs concerning the afterlife. Describing a journey through Inferno (hell), Purgatorio (purgatory), and Paradiso (heaven), the poem makes substantial use of the leading themes of Christian theology and spirituality, culminating with heaven, the ultimate goal of the Christian life. Dante portrayed the geography of hell as consisting of nine successive levels, each circle exponentially greater in torture and pain. The first circle, populated with virtuous non-Christians such as Aristotle, Seneca, and Virgil, was a place called "limbo," seen as a kind of "ante-hell," where no pain is experienced. Dante's work, written during an age when society and human life were precarious and under constant threat, helped establish medieval perceptions of the afterlife.

During the Enlightenment, many if not all Christian doctrines came under intense scrutiny. Enlightenment thinkers viewed belief in the afterlife as superstition and wish fulfillment, a projection of human longing for rewards and retribution. They particularly attacked the idea of eternal punishment, since it seemed to serve no useful purpose. The twentieth century, however, saw a rediscovery of eschatology. Though the doctrine's revival can be attributed to a number of factors, it was primarily due to a general collapse in confidence concerning human goodness and human civilization. The First World War, especially traumatic, was followed by the Great Depression and the terrors of Nazism, leading to the Holocaust and the threat of nuclear war. These events and related concerns raised doubts among Christians concerning the credibility of the liberal humanist vision and led to renewed stress on their eschatological beliefs, characterized by apocalyptic solutions focused on the rapture of believers to heaven and the punishment of unbelievers in hell.

Despite the residue of apocalypticism in twenty-first-century America, exacerbated in part by the global war against terrorism and other ongoing threats to our well-being, it is hard to imagine that any reflective person today believes in a literal doctrine of hell. It should be obvious by now that all traditional images of the afterlife, including heaven and hell, are born of fertile human minds.

Is there life after death? We cannot know for sure. While most biblical passages on this topic represent the early believers' apocalyptic hope, one passage rings true for me, keeping open the door to the afterlife: "No eye has seen, nor ear heard, nor the human heart conceived, what God has prepared for those who love him" (1 Cor. 2:9).

Apocalyptic Perspectives in the Bible

In the Bible, teaching concerning salvation and the afterlife is very much a part of its eschatological perspective. Eschatology is the study of final things, including the resurrection of the dead, the Last Judgment, the defeat of evil, the end of this world, and the creation of a new one. A fully formed eschatology with all of these features emerged only late in the development of biblical traditions.

The classic prophets of Israel were mostly concerned with the events of history, speaking boldly and without compromise against current disobedience and disbelief within the social, religious, and political establishment. Biblical prophets rarely, if ever, made open predictions about the future, and when they did so, the predictions were linked to their role as social critics, which focused on the consequences for unrepentance. The prophet's futuristic role was associated primarily with the certainty of the coming of the Lord, a coming to make things right through judgment and reward.

Toward the end of the sixth century BC, after the Jews returned from the Babylonian captivity, they held on to the prophetic hopes and visions, longing for a time when they could function once again under theocratic ideals. During the postexilic period, the prophetic expectation expanded to include messianic hope, longing for the arrival of God's kingdom. But the kingdom of God did not materialize, and messianic hope had to be deferred.

As time went on, some persecuted members of the Jewish community became pessimistic about an earthly kingdom of God and looked for salvation from above through direct intervention from God. This led to the development of apocalyptic eschatology, postexilic passages added to the book of Isaiah dubbed the Isaianic apocalypse (Isa. 24–27) and Third Isaiah (Isa. 56–66). These passages speculate about end-time events, including the Lord's arrival as king on Mount Zion, the judgment of the nations accompanied by heavenly portents, the abolition of death, the resurrection of the dead, the destruction of Leviathan (the chaos monster), and the creation of a new heaven and a new earth.

Like the prophets, apocalyptists expected an end followed by a new era of God's saving activity. But the apocalyptists saw the end as complete and final. The judgment would be not only on Israel but on all nations. This judgment would include not only their earthly foes but the cosmic forces of evil as well.

Many of these elements appear in the New Testament, for early Christianity inherited its eschatological framework from Judaism. To understand Jesus and the Gospels, scholars suggest three eschatological perspectives: (1) "consistent eschatology," meaning that Jesus' eschatological teachings as presented in the Gospels refer only to what will happen at the end of the world; (2) "realized eschatology," meaning that Jesus understood the anticipated kingdom of God to have arrived with himself; and (3) "inaugurated eschatology," meaning that Jesus brought the dawning of the awaited kingdom. This latter view finds some aspects of God's reign to be present in Jesus, but other elements of the kingdom would not appear until the very end. It is clear from passages such as the Synoptic Apocalypse (see Mark 13; Matt. 24–25; and Luke 21), where signs of the end are given, that Jesus believed the fullness of the kingdom would arrive shortly, probably within his generation (see Mark 13:30).

For the writers of the New Testament, Jesus' followers are situated between the inauguration of the kingdom of God and its consummation. In the meantime, they are to be busy preaching the gospel, doing good works, and modeling exemplary lives.

Jesus and the Presence of the Kingdom

The dominant theme in the preaching of Jesus—indeed the center of his mission and message—is the coming of the kingdom of God. While the phrase "kingdom of God" is rare in contemporary Jewish writings, it is widely regarded as one of the most distinctive aspects of the preaching of Jesus. Because almost everywhere in the Old Testament the idea of the kingdom is related to the people of Israel and the rule of the house of David in Jerusalem, Jesus is at pains to divest his teaching of this former understanding of the nature of the kingdom. What Jesus proclaims is the immediate sovereignty of God, who will take control of the destinies of all humans, restore humanity to what God had intended it to be, and overthrow the evil powers that had led astray human beings from their proper destiny.

In Mark's Gospel, Jesus' first act upon returning from his sojourn in the wilderness is to proclaim the coming of the kingdom (1:15). Here Jesus is picking up where Second Isaiah left off half a millennium earlier. Isaiah had envisioned a day when God would finally bring justice to the world, when the long-suffering faithful could rejoice at the end of oppression. Jesus shared Isaiah's anticipation but was more specific about when this time would come: "Truly I tell you, there are some standing here who will not taste death until they see that the kingdom of God has come with power" (Mark 9:1). His audience was to repent and "believe in the good news."

Whatever Jesus envisioned in his proclamation about the kingdom, it was going to be on earth. Despite Matthew's preference for the expression, "kingdom of heaven," it is clear that the concept, as Jesus used it, refers to the destiny of good people on a new, improved earth. It has nothing to do with the souls of dead people ascending to heaven.

In New Testament teaching the coming of the kingdom is always dependent on divine initiative, never on human achievement. Humans may enter the kingdom; they may proclaim it and inherit it (Matt. 25:34; 7:21), but they can neither earn it nor bring it forth. Because the word "kingdom" suggests a geographical region or realm, which is misleading in this context, scholars prefer the term "kingship" or "kingly rule of God."

The term "kingdom" is complex and paradoxical at its core. In the Synoptic Gospels, the paradoxical nature of the kingdom is manifested in several ways: (a) it is present (Matt. 12:28; Luke 17:21), yet not fully present (Matt. 8:29; 13:30); (b) it is a gift (Matt. 25:34; Luke 12:32), yet it also involves human effort (Matt. 6:33; Luke 12:31); (c) it is an internal reality (Luke 17:20–21), yet it has external implications for the world (Matt. 6:10). Scholars are particularly interested in the first of these, for it addresses the tension between the present time and the future, the "already" and the "not yet." In that regard, they have introduced the term "inaugurated eschatology" to refer to the relation of the present inauguration and the future fulfillment of the kingdom.

There is a present element in the New Testament concept of the kingdom, particularly in the teaching of Jesus, which is colored by a sense of intense urgency. God has already taken the initiative; humans are challenged to recognize the reality of the present situation and to make such decisions as will qualify them to become citizens of the kingdom. The signs of the presence of the kingdom are already present in the ministry of Jesus. When John the Baptist questions the mission of Jesus and asks for signs, he is given clear evidence: "the blind receive their sight, the lame walk, the lepers are cleansed, the deaf hear, the dead are raised, and the poor have good news brought to them" (Matt. 11:5). All these are signs that the power of the kingdom is presently at work. Those who refuse to recognize that the power evident in Jesus is a power from God are told: "if it is by the finger of God that I cast out the demons, then the kingdom of God has come to you" (Luke 11:20). When one person, for a period of some thirty-five years, lives in total dependence upon God, with a unique understanding of God's will and in unconditional surrender to it, the kingdom is already present. As Jesus tells the Pharisees in answer to their question about when the kingdom was coming: "the kingdom of God is among you" (Luke 17:21).

According to the New Testament, Christians are kind of hybrid creatures who live in two dimensions. They are citizens of the present age while at the same time living under the dominion of Christ's kingdom. As Paul put it somewhat paradoxically, Christians live "in the flesh" (human nature) and also "in the Spirit" (the new dimension introduced by Christ). Awareness of this dual citizenship led early Christians to say that they were "strangers" in the historical era on earth (Heb. 11:13). Ever since the New Testament period, Christianity has had to steer between two dangers: the temptation (1) to withdraw from society on the assumption that Christ's kingdom is not of this world (John 18:36), and (2) to make a too easy identification of the kingdom with something in this world, such as the institutional church or the ideal human society. However, the essential message of the New Testament is this: The kingdom is not of this world, yet it has been manifest in this world through the life, death, and resurrection of Christ. Although God's kingdom is a higher order than any political reality or human ideal of the present age, it has influenced and penetrated the kingdoms of this world—not as a tangent touches a circle but as a vertical line intersects a horizontal plane. The task of the church is to bear witness to this "vertical dimension" of history and, in so doing, to seek to leaven and redeem society in the name of Christ. This attitude toward society is not one of "detachment" but of "transfiguration," involving a rhythm of withdrawal and return through worship and action, faith and good works.

The tension between the "already" and the "not yet" nature of the kingdom is evident also in Paul's eschatology. At several points Paul emphasizes that the coming of Jesus inaugurates a new era or "age," which he designates a "new creation" (2 Cor. 5:17). While the presence of this new age can already be experienced, for Paul the ultimate transformation of the world is yet to come. Viewing the resurrection of Jesus as eschatological event, for it confirms that the "new age" is truly present, Paul also looks ahead to the future coming of Jesus Christ in judgment at the end of time. Another theme of Paul's eschatology is the coming of the Holy Spirit. This theme, which builds on a long-standing aspect of Jewish expectation, sees the gift of the Spirit as a confirmation that the new age has dawned in Christ. One of the most significant aspects of Paul's thought is his interpretation of the gift of the Spirit to believers as a "guarantee" or "first installment" of ultimate salvation (2 Cor. 1:22; 5:5).

Realized Eschatology in John's Gospel

A life with God is possible in the present even though that final life in all its fullness has not yet arrived. There is a tension in John's Gospel, and indeed throughout the New Testament, between "the already and the not yet." Passages such as John 3:17–21, 31–36, and 6:47 exemplify realized eschatology meaning that God's long-awaited eschatological transformation of reality, including judgment of evil and reward of faith (eternal life), is underway in the present, initiated by Jesus' coming into the world. The very presence of Jesus in the world confronts the world with a decision, to believe or not to believe, and making that decision is the moment of judgment. If one's life is characterized by transformative belief, so that one's deeds are "done in God"

(3:21), then one is saved; if one does not believe, one is already condemned. John's Gospel does include traditional understandings of eschatology and the final judgment (5:28–29; 12:48), but judgment and eternal life as present realities are at the theological heart of the Fourth Gospel.

It is crucial for the Evangelist (a reference, in this case, to the author of the Fourth Gospel) that God's judgment of the world arises out of God's love for the world. When God sent Jesus, God presented the world with a critical moment of decision. In each person's decision whether to accept God's offer of salvation, the world judges itself. Decision and self-judgment define Johannine eschatology. In New Testament scholar Rudolf Bultmann's eloquent words, the Fourth Gospel expresses "a radical understanding of Jesus' appearance as the eschatological event. This event puts an end to the old course of the world. From now on there are only believers and unbelievers, only saved and lost, those who have life and who are in death. This is because the event is grounded in the love of God, that love which gives life to faith, but which must become judgment in the face of unbelief."[5]

As the Evangelist believed in eternal life as something already present for the followers of Jesus, so he also believed in realized wrath, that God's wrath is already present for those who reject and disobey God. For John, there are always moral consequences to one's actions, both sooner and later.

"Eternal life," the term John uses instead of "kingdom of God," is not something believers possess only after death. It begins as soon as one places trust in Jesus as God's Son. Contemporary Christians have become so used to associating eternal life with going to heaven that the idea of realized eschatology, which views the future as somehow present now, seems perplexing. The notion of "eternal life," like "kingdom of God," is paradoxical at its core. Eternal life, like the kingdom of God, (a) is already present, yet not fully so. This becomes clearer when we understand that "eternal life" has as much to do with the quality and direction of life as with the length of one's existence. A better term might be "everlasting life," meaning a life that begins for believers in this lifetime but continues on forever. Eternal life (b) is a gift of God, yet it requires belief and is validated by bearing good fruit; and eternal life (c) has a spiritual nature, yet is related to physical existence. According to Pauline expectation, human existence will continue in bodily form ("further clothed"; 2 Cor. 5:4) after death.

When Jesus was quoted in John's Gospel as saying that he had come to give others life, and give it abundantly (10:10), he was speaking of eternal

---

5. Bultmann, *John*, 159.

life as a present reality. He was divulging his grandest teaching: We already have eternal life. Jesus affirmed and his immediate followers confirmed that the kingdom of God was a present reality (Luke 17:21). The human quest for eternal life is not based on the claim that one might live after death, but rather on an awareness that self-conscious human life already shares in the eternity of God. Eternal life is experienced in the present to the degree that one is in communion with that life-enhancing power of love we call God. Meister Eckhart, the medieval mystic, claimed that the highest parting for humans comes when "for God's sake we take leave of God." While we cannot be sure what Eckhart had in mind, one way to construe his enigmatic expression is to shift our image of God from one who is external to one who is internal, recognizing that we are already "in God." To embrace this recognition is to experience what the Bible calls "eternal life."

If there will be a new heaven and a new earth, as the book of Revelation indicates, if God's kingdom will one day fully manifest itself on earth, as Matthew indicates, and if there will be a future resurrection, as 1 Corinthians 15 declares, then Christians must be concerned not only about heavenly things but also about earthly things—for all creation shall one day be redeemed (Rom. 8:19–20). No one should be more concerned about caring for the earth and matters of global import than Christians, since our concerns are evidently God's concern as well. God not only made creation, God loves creation, and is in the process of redeeming it. It is an impoverished vision of the gospel "that cares for the souls of the unsaved but not their bodies or minds, that cares for heaven but not the conditions on earth, that cares for spiritual things but not also material things."[6]

Rethinking Heaven

While boundaries exist between heaven and earth, future and present, deity and humanity, and good and evil, there is dynamism to boundaries in the Bible. Boundaries do not fix limits beyond which it is impossible to pass. Rather they locate the place where transformations occur, allowing a flow across planes, eras, social categories, or moral values.

In the book of Revelation, "heaven" is the starting point for all revelation. John is taken into God's throne room so that he can see "behind the scenes" and understand how things fit together. "[A]nd there in heaven a door stood open" (4:1); this perspective is vital to the message of Revelation.

---

6. Witherington, *John's Wisdom*, 113.

John's cosmological perspective should be interpreted spiritually, not spatially. Going to "heaven," in John's vision, is less about cosmic geography and more about the place where God chooses to reveal himself, the place where heavenly realities are made plain. Heaven offers a divine perspective concerning events on earth, a new way of seeing that is beyond the control of earthly rulers. Heaven is the deeper dimension that offers God's perspective on what happens on earth.

We should not, however, restrict "heaven" to the spiritual dimension of reality, for it represents more than that. What John sees in heaven is not simply divine perspective. Heaven represents what is right and good and proper. When Jesus tells his followers to pray, "Your kingdom come . . . on earth as it is in heaven" (Matt. 6:10), he understands "heaven" not as a future destination for humans but as God's dimension of everyday reality. Heaven is in charge; heaven takes the lead; heaven represents what ought to be happening on earth. Every moment of each day is a unique point of contact with the divine. The eternal now is God's great gift to humanity. As Elizabeth Barrett Browning wrote:

> Earth's crammed with heaven,
> And every common bush afire with God;
> And he who sees it takes off his shoes--
> The rest sit round it and pluck blackberries.[7]

The Second Coming of Christ and the End of History

The world as we know it will end; that is a scientific fact. However, if someone tells you they know when history will end or how it will end, or provides details concerning the second coming of Christ, pay no attention, for such knowledge is not given to mortals.

In the Bible, much of the language about the future is couched in eschatological or apocalyptic imagery. It flows from the hopes and fears of first-century believers living under oppressive Roman rule. Such imagery is imaginative and speculative; it is not predictive, and should not be taken literally.

Throughout history and in our time as well there have been bold and detailed predictions about the end time, and all have proven wrong. Scripture warns us about false prophets and teachers (see Matt. 24:11–13)

---

7. *Aurora Leigh*, Book VII, line 820.

and exhorts every generation to focus on the present rather than on the unknown future. In the week before his crucifixion, Jesus cautioned his disciples not to speculate about situations of uncertainty: "But about that day and hour no one knows, neither the angels of heaven, nor the Son, but only the Father" (Matt. 24:36). Earlier, when teaching about prayer, Jesus had exhorted his disciples to focus on earthly realities while praying for daily needs (see the Lord's Prayer in Matt. 6:10–11).

In the book of Acts, the resurrected Jesus counters the disciples' request for a timetable of end-time events with timely advice: "It is not for you to know such things. Your goal is to be faithful with the opportunities at hand. For this task you will be empowered by God's Holy Spirit" (Acts 1:7–8 paraphrased). The apostle Paul encourages his readers with similar advice: "Finally, beloved, whatever is true, whatever is honorable, whatever is just, whatever is pure, whatever is pleasing, whatever is commendable . . ., think about these things. Keep on doing the things that you have learned and received and heard and seen . . ." (Phil. 4:8–9).

We hear much nowadays in the media about "the rapture of believers to heaven" before the great tribulation on earth. We should not succumb to such speculation, for the word "rapture" is not biblical, and the concept represents a misinterpretation of scripture. While scripture tells us to await the coming of Christ, it is more helpful to think of Christ's return as an ongoing reality that empowers us in the present, rather than as a singular event awaited in the future. In some passages of the Bible, the emphasis is on the ongoing coming of Christ into the lives of believers, bringing to every generation the promise of God's power and presence. When, in John's Gospel, the resurrected Jesus bestowed the Holy Spirit on the disciples (see John 20:22), Jesus unleashed resurrection power on present and future followers. With that empowerment, the focus shifted from the old to the new, from the anticipated future to the proleptic present. The marching orders are clear: "As the Father has sent me, so I send you." For those in Christ, for those in the Spirit, the future is now (see Paul's realized eschatology in 2 Cor. 5:17). Together, we are God's anticipated future!

The book of Revelation sets the record straight. Christians are not raptured to heaven to escape the sufferings of earth. The author knows nothing of a "rapture" of believers to escape earthly tribulation. Rather, Christians are to conquer on earth through suffering and death, as Jesus did. The church's experience of being called by God is not to escape from this earth. Christians are not spared trials and tribulations, but rather experience

God's presence and care *through* life's struggles. At the end of Revelation, humans are not translated to a celestial realm, for God dwells on earth; and where God is, there is heaven. Instead of envisioning the followers of Christ as "raptured" from earth, it is more helpful to think of them as the ones who are "left behind," that is, who are called to embody God's kingdom and its values on earth. Contrary to ideas about the "rapture" of the church from earth at the second coming of Christ, there is no such "rapture" in Revelation. Instead, it is God who is "raptured" to earth to live with us.

The Bible tells us not to worry about the unknown future, for it is secure in God's hands. Christians need not live by fear, but rather by faith in the certainty of God's unconditional love. If someone fears punishment because he or she has broken God's commandments, God's remedy is clear. It appears all throughout scripture, but perhaps most clearly in three passages:

1. In John 3:16 we learn that the "world" (in John's Gospel this is a term not simply for the created order but for the realm of doubt and disbelief) is the object of God's love. Unlike human love, God's love is not possessive or selective. God does not simply love those who are converts, or who are "born again," or who love God in return. Rather, in Christ God so loved the sinful world that God gave the very best: Godself. If people act in evil and hurtful ways because they belong to the world and its values, how can such evil be overcome? John's answer sounds simple, but it represents what Christian theologian Dietrich Bonhoeffer termed "costly grace": by walking in the light, a form of discipleship described as living life abundantly (John 10:10). While it sounds simple, the journey from darkness to light requires continuous transformation of the self, a process John entrusts to the Holy Spirit.

2. In 1 John 4:18 we learn that "there is no fear in love, but perfect love casts out fear." God's remedy for fear, guilt, and wrongdoing is not punishment or self-recrimination but love: love for God and love for others. Surprisingly, in such loving, the starting point is not the former but the latter. By loving family members, neighbors, and those in need here on earth, we demonstrate our love for God: "If we love one another, God lives in us, and his love is perfected in us" (1 John 4:12).

3. In James 1:27 we learn that practical love, not mystical or heroic love, defines true religion: "Religion that is pure and undefiled . . . is this:

to care for orphans and widows in their distress, and to keep oneself unstained by the [self-centered, unbelieving] world."

Reverse the Curse

What would happen to your faith—and your perspectives, priorities, lifestyle, even your attitudes—if you took as theological starting point the reality of original goodness ("original blessing") rather than original sin? The fall-redemption spiritual tradition, also known as "the heaven-and-hell framework," has dominated Christian anthropology, theology, biblical studies, theological education, and even sociology for centuries. The fall-redemption model, based on patriarchal models that are dualistic and outdated, comprises four central elements: the afterlife, sin and forgiveness, Jesus' death for the sin of humanity, and belief.

According to this model, heaven is the goal of life, the primary reason for being Christian. Sin is the central issue in one's life, and forgiveness is the solution. Because humans are sinners, they deserve to be punished. But Jesus died for our sins, thereby making forgiveness possible. Those who affirm ("believe in") this framework and accept ("have faith in") Christ's gift of forgiveness are assured eternal life with God in heaven. The fall-redemption framework, which is closely aligned with the Precritical Paradigm, views the Christian life as centered in belief now for the sake of eternal salvation. What is most important about Jesus is not his life but his death, and belief in him is central to one's eternal salvation. The goal of life is a blessed afterlife, which can only be gained through Christ's work of salvation, received by faith, and maintained through worship and the sacramental life.

Critics view the fall-redemption model as guilt-ridden and therefore as psychologically flawed, in that it tends to devalue life and deprive it of much of its vitality, joy, and goodness. This framework is also said to be based on a false and unbiblical meaning of key concepts such as salvation, sacrifice, mercy, repentance, redemption, and faith, which in the Bible are concerned with temporal safety, peace, and wellbeing and rarely refer to heaven or the afterlife. In addition, this perspective is viewed by many historians and theologians as having adversely contributed to racism, sexism, nationalism, exclusivism, and other harmful ideologies.[8]

---

8. For additional information on the "heaven-and-hell framework" and on how

By contrast, the creation-centered tradition, which is more ancient, emphasizes goodness, blessing, joy, creativity, play, innocence, and pleasure rather than sin and guilt, and is committed to social transformation and justice-making. Because the fall/redemption tradition considers all nature "fallen" and does not seek God in nature but inside the individual soul, it tends to ignore science or be hostile to it.

According to theologian Matthew Fox, author of *Original Blessing* and other creation-centered books: "To recover a spiritual tradition in which the goodness of creation and the study of creation matters would be to inaugurate new possibilities between spirituality and science that would shape the paradigms for culture, its institutions, and its people. These paradigms would be powerful in their capacity to transform. For if wisdom comes from nature and religious traditions . . . then what might happen if science and religious traditions agreed to birth together instead of ignoring, fighting, or rejecting one another? Is not recovering a creation-centered spirituality recovering two sources of wisdom at once, that of nature via science and that of nature via religious traditions? The creation-centered tradition seems to combine the best of both worlds in our search for wisdom today."[9]

Reconfiguring Christianity's predominant dogmatic paradigm—replacing the fall/redemption model with the creation-centered model—can make a great difference in one's faith and lifestyle. Our focus as Christians should be on the here-and-now, on our "this-worldly" task and journey. In my estimation, focusing on sin as a path to damnation and on salvation as a path to the afterlife is peripheral to Christianity and serves as a distraction from the urgent tasks at hand. Furthermore, to quote award-winning author Robert Wright, "religions that have failed to align individual salvation with social salvation have not, in the end, fared well. And, like it or not, the social system to be saved is now a global one. Any religion whose prerequisites for individual salvation don't conduce to the salvation of the whole world is a religion whose time has passed."[10]

---

particular Christian words have lost their original meaning and power, see Borg, *Speaking Christian*, 10–17.

9. Fox, *Original Blessing*, 11–12.

10. Wright, *Evolution of God*, 430.

Going Deeper: Reflection for Participants

1. What benefits can the Spirit model of God bring to Christians fragmented and polarized over doctrines such as sin and salvation?
2. Discuss and assess the meaning of "atonement theology." Of the various interpretations given regarding the meaning of the cross in the New Testament, which do you find most compelling? Why?
3. In his discussion on salvation, Alistair McGrath posits various answers to the questions: "From what are we saved"? and "For what are we saved"? Which of his answers do you find most valid? Why?
4. Assess the merits of the author's statement that "images of the afterlife, including heaven and hell, are born of fertile minds."
5. Discuss the differences between prophetic and apocalyptic views of reality and of evil.
6. Is there a timetable for earthly history? If so, is it under divine, human, or natural control?
7. John's Gospel, the last canonical Gospel written and the most spiritual, teaches that eternal life is a present reality and not simply a longing for life after death. How might the notion of "realized eschatology" influence the way you live in the present?
8. Discuss what you learned from this chapter about heaven and eternal life.
9. In your estimation, will human history on earth end shortly or will it continue indefinitely into the unknown future? Should we be optimistic or pessimistic about human destiny?
10. Compare and contrast the "fall/redemption" paradigm (redemption theology) with the "creation spirituality" paradigm. Which of the two do you find most compelling? Why?
11. In your estimation, what is the primary insight gained from this session?

Session 10

Rethinking the Church, Its Nature, Mission, and Composition
Exclusive or Inclusive, Homogeneous or Heterogeneous?

Getting Started

Homework Assignment: Answer the following questions, writing your answers in your journal. Be prepared to share your views with others in the class. 1. Is the church primarily a conserving organization or a liberating organization? 2. Should local churches strive for the unity and like-mindedness of their members, for diversity and inclusivity of their membership, or somehow aspire equally for both? Support your answer. 3. After finishing this chapter, reread the appendix. Have you grown in your faith during this study? If so, how? As a result of this study, have you reached a new phase in Fowler's stages of faith (see the appendix)? Explain your answer.

Gaining Momentum

Starting theological discussions with the Spirit model rather than the monarchical model of God affects the meaning not only of what we believe, but also changes how we live. It does so by changing the framework in which things are seen. In this session we will explore how the Spirit model of God transforms our understanding of the doctrine of the church.

The images of God associated with the Spirit model dramatically affect how we think of the Christian life. Rather than God as a distant judge with whom we might spend eternity—if we are good enough, accept Jesus, or get with the program—the Spirit model emphasizes that God (the sacred) is always present. Rather than sin and guilt being the central dynamic of the Christian life, the central dynamic becomes relationship—with God, the world, and each other. The monarchical model promotes stability, security, conformity, and uniformity, while the Spirit model promotes newness, growth, change, and transformation.

Corporate Personality

If we are to understand the Christian doctrine of the church, we need to become familiar with the biblical concept of corporate personality. The Bible portrays Israel as God's people, not simply a collection of persons but a divine company ("a priestly kingdom and a holy nation"; Exod. 19:5; 1 Pet. 2:9). Out of families, clans, and tribes God formed a nation, with a corporate personality: When one person suffered, everyone suffered; when one person was blessed, the people enjoyed the benefits; when one person sinned, the whole nation participated in the judgment; when one person received a promise, he or she did so on behalf of the nation.

Americans today live in an individualistic and pluralistic society, with diverse cultures, religions, and societal values. Ancient societies were quite the opposite; they were homogeneous, with little tolerance or diversity, and with no such thing as freedom of religion. The concept of corporate personality provided Israel with stability, solidarity, and unity during the period of its ascendency. These qualities enabled Israelites to maintain social and religious cohesion in a sea of paganism. Their laws, rituals, and values provided them with a distinctive way of life, which has preserved the Jewish people to this day. In order to be a community the Israelites needed land—physical and geographical space where they could carry out their theocratic uniqueness—and a temple—where they could make their pilgrimage, bring their tithes and offerings, and celebrate their festivals.

To understand the biblical concept of community one must begin with Abraham. God started with one family, declaring a promise so wondrous yet absurd as to engender laughter, creating something in Sarah's womb when she was unable to conceive: "Is anything too wonderful for the Lord?" (Gen. 18:14). From Isaac came Jacob, and from him the twelve tribes of

Israel. They took his name, his personality, his style of life, and the covenant he had with God. They would call themselves "*bene* Israel," sons of Israel. The doctrine of election was not arbitrary. Rather it reminded them that they were beloved, God's intentional creation. They were not one nation *out of* many, but one nation *for* many. In such unity there is resolve, resilience, and strength.

The Journey of Faith: Three Levels of Existence

Søren Kierkegaard, the noted Christian existentialist, made an important contribution to the religious journey in his formulation of three levels of existence or stages through which humans go in their ascent toward God. On the first level, which he labeled the aesthetic stage, individuals are ruled by their senses. Such persons live solely for the present, and particularly for self-gratification. The second level, the ethical stage, requires that one abandon attitudes of selfishness and embrace universal standards, making commitments to others. Here moral standards and obligations are adopted as dictated by reason. The third and final stage, which Kierkegaard called the religious stage, entails a life of faith.

In each stage, Kierkegaard selected a figure from literature or history as an example. For the model of the religious stage of life, the highest level through which humans go in their ascent toward God, he selected Abraham, whose trust of God and unwavering obedience led him to choose to sacrifice his only son Isaac, even in the face of absurdity, for to question God would be to place reason over faith. In selecting this example, Kierkegaard was not denying the validity of ethics. He stated that the individual who is called to break with the ethical must first be ethical, that is, must first have subordinated to universal morality. The break, when one is called to make it, is made in "fear and trembling" and not arrogantly or proudly. In this final stage, the ethical is not abolished but dethroned by a higher purpose or end, a phenomenon he described as the "teleological suspension of the ethical." The key to this final stage is not the commendable humanistic goal of universal duty to others, but the unqualified giving of oneself to God. For Kierkegaard, if one doesn't go beyond the ethical realm, beyond moral obligation, one cannot properly say that one is related to God, or obedient to God. Ethical duty, he believed, must ultimately lead to God, but since it usually leads to humanity (i.e. to humanism), then this stage must be transcended. An absolute relationship to an absolute (God) requires a relative relationship to relative ends. And for Kierkegaard, everything other than God is relative.

In the nineteenth century Kierkegaard was a voice crying in the wilderness of a complacent civilization, for his one passion was to show what it meant to be a Christian. The church in his day was so institutionalized, he argued, that it was no longer Christian; in fact, it had become "impossible to be a Christian in Christendom."

For some Christians today the journey of faith is a solitary sojourn, an existential experience. They may be introverted, shy, or simply mystics. Their Christianity is an extension of their individualism, their faith characterized by devotion. They are concerned with personal growth and the transformation of the self. When they serve others, they do so out of love for God. For other Christians, the journey of faith is a shared sojourn, a communal experience. Their Christianity is an extension of their social nature, their faith characterized by duty. Service with and for others comes naturally to them. Their pilgrimage requires fellowship, for they find in the community of believers their identity and belonging. Both ways of being Christian are legitimate, because they belong together. The church was designed for both order and ardor, for personal piety and social cohesion. When Jesus called disciples, he called them to relate to him individually, but he also called them to discipleship, to the fellowship of believers.

When I ponder the Christian life—the journey of faith—I recall a valuable insight from the Second World War, when ships would often leave port with nothing to guide them but a set of coordinates in an envelope. When the ship arrived at those coordinates, there would be a second envelope, with another set of coordinates, and so on. These ships were sailing under sealed orders.

That's when I remember Abraham. Why would anyone want to leave Mesopotamia, especially a city such as Ur, with three-story houses, a great harbor, and the promise of a successful career? The only reason would be if God so seized him that he became willing to go forth without knowing where. That's the essence of faith, isn't it, traveling under sealed orders, sojourning from point to point. The Scriptures tell us that Abraham was the first person to have faith in God—to believe in God, to trust God implicitly.

Anyone who is growing is on a journey:

- From infancy to maturity.
- From love of self to love of neighbor.

- From ego-centrism to eco-centrism.
- From dogmatism to humility (meaning teachability, openness, and winsomeness).
- From ignorance to wisdom.

In the Bible, the prototypical model for the journey of faith is found in the patriarchal stories of Genesis 12--50, starting with the story of Abraham. It soon becomes evident that the underlying significance of chapters 12--50 is not the stories of the patriarchs but the story of Israel's self-understanding. At the time this material was put into writing, the main question was not, "Who are Abraham, Isaac, Jacob, and Joseph?" but "Who is Israel?" Israel was grappling with her identity, her self-understanding as a people called by God. The theological answer was found in the doctrine of election.

The Doctrine of Election

What does election mean? The biblical answer is given in the portrayal of Abraham, Isaac, and Jacob, patriarchs whose lives were characterized by the following traits:

1. They *lived by faith in God*. In Abraham, Israel understands something about herself, that she has been called into existence by God himself, that she has been created by God's initiative and preserved by God's grace. This would become a dominant theme during the Babylonian exile (see Isa. 41:8–10).

2. They were *called to be a servant people*. Election does not mean that one people is chosen because they are better than others, but rather that they are called to spread God's grace. God's purpose is seen in Genesis 12:3 ("in you all the families of the earth shall be blessed"); it is a universal purpose, one that moves from particulars to universals, from individuals to communities and nations. In Abraham, God brings one person of faith into existence in order that God's blessing might be extended to all humanity. This is the Bible's stress on election, that when God calls a people, they are called to service, and the rest of the Old Testament, and then the Gospels and epistles, show what it means to be a servant people. The Bible makes it clear that Israel's calling is part of God's healing intention (the biblical word for

healing, health, wholeness, and goodness is "salvation," like the Hebrew word "Shalom"). In the Bible, the election of a people becomes the basis for good news, what the New Testament calls "gospel." This is the message of Genesis 12--50, and it is transported to a higher key in the New Testament.

3. They were *called to a life of pilgrimage*—a life of mobility, movement, and change. Biblical faith is a calling faith, a calling to go forth, to be on the way, to be moving in God's direction, to be pioneers of faith. Abraham was told to break his ties with his land and his former security, a way of life that up to that point had been deeply rooted to the land. Like Abraham, God's people are called to a nomadic consciousness. We see that so clearly in the prophetic consciousness, a stance that could be counter-cultural in the sense that one could be both an agent of change and a critic of the established order. Their message was that God was doing a new thing. As we see in Abraham, faith is not so much consent or agreement as something dynamic, manifested in movement. So Abraham is the ancestor of a pilgrim people, as we learn in Hebrews 11, and his story highlights the themes of mobility and change, meaning that when faith becomes lifeless, stagnant, or frozen, whether into institutions with superiority complexes or into self-serving lifestyles, God breaks them down and forces his people into radical recommitment. The story of Abraham and the patriarchs is the story of God on the move with his people.

The Church as the New People of God

Every verse of the New Testament presupposes the new people of God, a new community called the church. From the beginning, Christians were characterized as "the body of Christ," followers of Jesus who showed by their lifestyle that they were a part of the new order that Jesus had announced and that they believed had now arrived. Theologically, the church was a microcosm of the transformation that God's new order would bring for the whole world. To be in the church was to have a foretaste of life as God's new people. Socially, the church in the Roman Empire was an alternative society, based not on selfishness and greed and exploitation, but on the new freedom and fellowship that Jesus had announced: freedom to love God and to love and serve others (Mark 12:29–31). As the church expanded across the Mediterranean world, it was indeed a new society—a context in which people of diverse social, racial, and religious backgrounds were united in a new and radical friendship. Because they had been reconciled to God, they found themselves reconciled to each other.[1]

Jesus conceived his mission to be that of calling the remnant of Israel—twelve disciples, corresponding to the twelve-tribe structure of Israel. And when the meaning of Jesus' life, death, and resurrection came upon these disciples with overwhelming power at the festival of Pentecost (Acts 2), a powerful movement emerged. This small community became a dynamic and militant church, with a message that "turned the world upside down" (Acts 17:6) and a gospel that was carried enthusiastically to the ends of the earth. The Acts of the Apostles gives the story of the emerging church. According to Acts, the church expanded because it fulfilled faithfully its two tasks in society: to evangelize, that is, to serve as Christ's witnesses "to the ends of the earth" (Acts 1:8; see also Matthew's Great Commission in Matt. 28:19-20), and to live by the ethics of love and mercy that Jesus had taught.

While stressing the newness of the church, we must also keep in mind the relation of this community to the entire Old Testament heritage. In a sense, the church may be called the "New Israel," for like ancient Israel, congregants had a special role in history. The Old Testament narrates how a people was formed to be the bearer of God's purpose in history and the instrument of God's saving work. Israel was not primarily a race or a nation but a covenant community created by God's action. Having delivered Israel from slavery in Egypt, God made them a covenant people. Through many tumultuous years, God educated and disciplined them in order that they might understand more deeply the meaning of their special role.

Second Isaiah understood most profoundly Israel's place in God's worldwide purpose. According to this prophet, Israel was called to be a "light to the nations" (Isa. 49:6) and a servant whose sufferings would benefit all humanity (Isa. 49:3; 53:4-6, 11-12). However, in the intervening years, this expansive vision was obscured. The last two centuries before Jesus witnessed a resurgence of Jewish nationalism that led in time to wars with Rome. In AD 70 the Romans destroyed the temple, leveled Jerusalem, and removed the last vestiges of Jewish statehood. So, in the fullness of time, God acted once again to reconstitute the community of Israel—no longer bound by ethnic or nationalistic limitations but open to all people, Jew and Gentile alike, on the basis of faith. The new community did not

---

1. Drane, *Introducing the New Testament*, 381-82.

establish a clean break with the people of God whose life story is portrayed in the Old Testament. Rather, as Paul puts it in his important discussion in Romans 9–11, the community is a "remnant chosen by grace." It is, so to speak, a "wild olive shoot" grafted onto the olive tree (Israel); and the "branch" (Gentile Christians) is supported by the roots that reach down deeply into God's choice of Israel and God's faithful dealings with this people (Rom. 11:17–24).

Although some parallels can be drawn with the ancient Hebrew cultic observances, the church in the New Testament takes quite a different form. It is more similar to the Jewish synagogue (a learning center) than to the temple and its cultic activities. At first, homes of believers served as the places of worship; only later did Christians build church structures comparable to Jewish synagogues. The cross became the central cultic object, rather than the Ark of the Covenant or Torah scrolls. The cross served as a sign of Jesus' crucifixion and resurrection and symbolized the meaning of these events. The first day of the week (Sunday), which commemorated Jesus' resurrection, replaced the Jewish Sabbath as the primary cultic season. In addition to the regular activities of worship and education, which helped to unify the new Christian community, the basic cultic acts were baptism and the Lord's Supper (the Eucharist).[2]

Such worship and religious practices did not emerge without problems, however, and new leaders were required. Initially, the disciples of Jesus (the Twelve) became prominent leaders of the Jerusalem church, with a smaller number—consisting of Peter, John, and James "the Just"—exercising greater influence. A somewhat larger group, known as apostles, became the preeminent figures in the spread of Christianity. This group included the Twelve, but the total company of apostles was more numerous. What made a person an apostle was a personal commission by Jesus (the Greek word *apostolos* means "one sent"). Apostles were ambassadors of the risen Lord, understood to have extraordinary authority in the church.

In the world beyond Jerusalem, the church generally assumed the form of a synagogue, that is, a congregation. The Greek word for church (*ekklēsia*) means a group of people called together. It is one of the words used in the Septuagint to designate the assembly of the people of Israel. Because the Jews chose the word *synagogē* for their assemblies, it is quite likely that the first Christians deliberately, and to avoid confusion, rejected the term adopted by the Jews and chose the other. Almost from the start, church

---

2. Bowne and Currid, "Biblical Society," 175.

congregations were governed by elders (Greek, *presbuteros*), one of whom was chief. With the passage of time, the office of chief elder evolved into that of bishop. Ephesians 4:11 lists prophets, evangelists, pastors, and teachers after apostles among the spiritually gifted leaders of the early church. Apostles stand first in 1 Corinthians 12:28, followed by prophets, teachers, miracle workers, healers, helpers, administrators, speakers in tongues, and interpreters. In keeping with the order of both lists, Paul assigned particular honor to the office of prophet (see 1 Cor. 14:1–19). While the authority of the apostle was derived from a connection with Jesus, that of the church prophet was entirely charismatic. As the church developed, the authority of the apostles was passed from the apostles to the bishops through apostolic succession, an authority initially not concerned with the passing of power but of correct teaching. Over time the charismatic offices in the church waned, whereas apostolic authority was deemed irreplaceable.

As developed by Paul, the church presupposes a faith community that is the source of social unity. All life, whether politics, economics, education, or religion, stands under the covenant relation to God. Within that conception, every believer has a part to play. Whether Christians meet together for worship or fellowship, all members are indispensable for all have something to contribute (see 1 Cor. 14:26–33). As a result, Paul asserts that every Christian has a distinct *charism*, a ministry that is not restricted by either ordination or some other special experience, but which is given to all by the work of the Spirit in the lives of believers (1 Cor. 12:7).

In the church, all members are of equal importance, and that includes equality of women with men. Because Paul's letters contain conflicting statements about the place of women in the church's life (due in part to later editorial activity), the recommended starting place for discovering Paul's own view is Galatians 3:28: "There is no longer Jew or Greek, there is no longer slave or free, there is no longer male and female; for all of you are one in Christ." Despite statements to the contrary, generally seen as interpolations (see 1 Cor. 14:33b–36) or post-Pauline (see 1 Tim. 2:11–15), the early Christian movement clearly affirmed sexual equality, prompting Thomas Cahill to call the primitive church "the world's first egalitarian society." Likewise, Cahill declares Paul's statement in 1 Corinthians 11:11 (that "in the Lord woman is not independent of man or man independent of woman") to be the clearest affirmation of sexual equality in the entire Bible—indeed, the first in world literature.[3] Paul happily worked along-

---

3. Cahill, *Desire of the Everlasting Hills*, 148.

side women, some of whom were his close friends (Phil. 4:2–3). His most extensive list of greetings to Christian leaders includes many women (Rom. 16:1–15), and he refers to at least one of them as "apostle" (Junia, Rom. 16:7). Furthermore, when Paul advises the church at Corinth about the appropriate way to behave, he takes it for granted that both men and women should pray or prophecy in public worship (1 Cor. 11:4–5). In 1 Corinthians 11:1–16 Paul uses rabbinic arguments where it suits him, moving in two directions simultaneously: conserving tradition by upholding the custom of head-covering, yet breaking with tradition in allowing women to participate in worship. The whole frame of reference is determined by Paul's insistence that men and women have the same freedom and opportunity to play a full part in the life of the church.

The same point also comes out clearly when Paul discusses marriage in 1 Corinthians 7. Some of what he writes is obscure, no doubt because of its specific reference to details of the Corinthian situation. But the general principle is clear: Men and women relate to each other not through domination but by mutual love and service.

For Paul what determines a person's function in the church is the endowment of God's Spirit. In God's new society, social distinctions such as gender, race, and social class are irrelevant. The heart of the gospel is freedom: freedom from guilt, from the Law, from sin, and from all that would inhibit the development of one's God-given potential. To be set free by Christ is to be released into a new world in which people can find their own true identity, relating to each other in freedom and fellowship because they are related to Christ himself. The final transformation, however, is yet in the future, when the "glorious freedom of the children of God" will be fully realized (Rom. 8:21). In the meantime, the church stands as a testimony to that future hope, and as the context in which people can serve one another as they love and serve God.

The Four Notes of the Church

Because the citizens of the kingdom belong to a community of believers and are not isolated individuals, they are responsible to maintain the four "notes" or marks of the church, that is, its four defining characteristics as noted in the creeds of Christendom:

- *One*: the unity of the church.

- *Holy*: the purity of the church (to be "holy" is to be set apart for and dedicated to service).
- *Catholic*: the universality of the church (every Christian is part of an inclusive and welcoming whole).
- *Apostolic*: the faithfulness of the church to its founding principles.

Through discipleship, the church models God's "new creation," exhibiting the presence of the kingdom of God to the world, thereby fulfilling individually and communally the cultural mandates associated with the covenant of creation (see Gen. 1:26—2:3). These ordinances, instituted for human wellbeing, include family, labor, and worship. The covenant of creation binds all humans to God and to one another. It entails that, as image-bearers, humans are to reflect God's concern for all of life.

Prayer: Vertical or Horizontal?

Because of its importance for individual as well as communal forms of worship, I close this session with a discussion of prayer. Prayer begins early in life. For some, it is the first religious act performed. While there are many forms of prayer, for most people prayer is petitionary, that is, it derives from something wanted, needed, or requested. Most of us were taught at an early age that God answers prayer. In the Bible we learn that when we are in need or in trouble, and we pray honestly, God hears and answers. And so we pray, sincerely. And if our prayer is noble, and not simply selfish, we expect God will answer in the affirmative.

As we grow up, we are troubled by ineffectual prayer; answers of conventional theology, such as "God said no" or "We can't know God's will," become troubling. At critical junctures in our lives, conventional answers raise storm clouds of doubt, and we wonder whether God answers prayer at all. We look at a world gone awry, where inequities and calamities befall innocent people, and we question God's justice and even God's reality.

One of the reasons why prayer has lost meaning for many is not spiritual ineptitude, but rather that the God to whom we had been taught to pray has been inadequate. Before one can raise new spiritual possibilities, one must become convinced of the bankruptcy of old theological paradigms. Note the problems with the Lord's Prayer, the model prayer recited by Christians in all times and places: "Our Father, who art in heaven. Hallowed be thy name" (Matt. 6:9; Luke 11:2). The depth of our separation from the God of the past becomes very apparent when we face the startling fact that we, in our time, cannot possibly begin in the same place where Jesus assumed that his disciples could begin.

Jesus' answer, for example, assumed that God was a person who could be addressed as "Father." He also assumed that this divine being was external to life, or "in heaven." Furthermore, he assumed that this male deity delighted in our recognition of the sacredness of his name. In addition, he suggested that this theistic God enjoyed the flattery of his subjects. These are all aspects of a theistic belief system that is no longer valid.

If we examine Jesus anew, and understand in him what Episcopal Bishop John Shelby Spong terms "a portrait of the presence of God in human life that manifests itself in wholeness," we have a basis for a new understanding of prayer. God represents wholeness, and if this is what God is, prayer is the experience of meeting that God. According to this understanding, prayer is:

- Being present with others, sharing love, opening life to transcendence. Prayer recognizes that there is a sacred core in every person that must not be violated.

- The conscious human intention to relate to the depths of life and love and thereby to be an agent of the creation of wholeness in another.

- The offering of our life and our love through the simple action of sharing our friendship and our acceptance. Prayer seeks the strength to give others the courage to dare, to risk, to be alive in a new way.

- The struggle for human justice. Prayer is our active opposition to those prejudices and stereotypes that diminish the personhood and the being of another.

- A call out of childish dependency into spiritual maturity.

- Being present, sharing love, opening to new possibilities. It is not necessarily words addressed heavenward. Prayer can never be separated from acting.[4]

Talking the Talk and Walking the Walk

For those interested in understanding how faith and practice interrelate, a good place to begin is the Sermon on the Mount, found in Matthew 5–7

4. Spong, *Christianity Must Change*, 143–48.

(an abbreviated and revised version appears in Luke's Sermon on the Plain; 6:17–49). The sermon, which incorporates some of Jesus' best-known teachings, ends with the powerful injunction that hearing and doing belong together. Those who know and do are likened to those who build their life upon a strong foundation, whereas those who know but do not do are likened to those who build on a weak foundation

The mission of the church is to serve the world that God loves unconditionally. Like God, the church is to be faithful and inclusive. Its role is to transform unbelievers to believers, and believers into doers, enabling them to talk the talk and walk the walk—simultaneously.

This is a unique moment in our world. In the face of new opportunities and a rapidly changing world, our nation is seeking to determine its nature and role. Our society and its institutions are floundering, uncertain of their identity. New leadership is needed, with new vision and renewed resolve. To rediscover its role as the salt and light company, the church needs to undergo reformation yet again, leading by example. The church needs to inspire the youth of the world, attracting the best to church vocations and lay ministry. The world is waiting for such a church, and when it appears, many will join. Like the first believers, such a church will turn the world upside down. Transfomed by God and energized by the Spirit model rather than the monarchical model of God, together we can help make our country's motto—"One nation under God"—a reality. When that church arises, God's eschatological kingdom will be realized yet again. We are the ones the world is waiting for. May you, dear reader, refined by fire, commit to that revolution.

Going Deeper: Reflection for Participants

1. What does this chapter say about corporate personality? What would you say to those who tell you that they have no need of the church because they can be Christian individually?

2. When thinking of the church's mission, should the focus be primarily on evangelism and indoctrination, on providing its members personal care and healing, on challenging social injustice, on creating opportunities for personal growth and transformation, or on all of the above? If you consider all important, how would you rank them?

3. Evaluate Kierkegaard's "religious stage." What merit do you find in his three-stage model for the religious journey?

4. What did Kierkegaard mean when he stated that it is "impossible to be a Christian in Christendom"? Do you agree with his assessment?

5. Does God exhibit national, racial, social, or sexual bias? If not, what about the doctrine of election? Does God favor some people, all people, or none? Support your answer.

6. What does this chapter say about the early church as a community?

7. Discuss the meaning of Thomas Cahill's statement that the early church was "the world's first egalitarian society." Does that reference hold true for today's church? Why or why not?

8. One of the four "notes" of the church is unity. If the church's responsibility is to unify people, not divide them (see Ps. 133:1), is this goal achievable in today's society? What can you say and do to bring about greater unity in your local church and in your local community?

9. If you were to prioritize the three qualities or "notes" of the church (peace, unity, and purity), what order would you give? Support your answer.

10. If the nature of Christianity has changed since its inception in a Jewish setting some two thousand years ago, what might the church look like a century from now?

11. In your estimation, what is the primary insight gained from this session?

Appendix

James Fowler's Stages of Faith

Stage 0: Primal Faith – (0 to 2 years): This stage is characterized by early learning the safety of the environment. Under consistent nurture, children develop a sense of safety about the universe and the divine. Negative experiences (neglect and abuse) lead to distrust of the universe and the divine.

Stage 1: *Intuitive-Projective* – (3 to 7 years): This is the stage of preschool children in which fantasy and reality often are mixed together. However, during this stage, our most basic ideas about God are usually learned from our parents and/or society.

Stage 2: *Mythic-Literal* – (mostly in school children): When children become school-age, they start understanding the world in more logical ways. They generally accept the stories told to them by their faith community but tend to understand them in very literal ways. [A few people remain in this stage through adulthood.]

Stage 3: *Synthetic-Conventional* – (arising in adolescence; ages 12 to adulthood): Most people move on to this stage as teenagers. At this point, their lives have grown to include several different social circles, which they need to pull together. When this happens, a person usually adopts some sort of all-encompassing belief system. However, at this stage, people tend to have a hard time seeing outside their box, not recognizing that they are "inside" a belief system. At this stage, authority is usually placed in individuals or groups that represent one's beliefs. [In this many people remain.]

Stage 4: *Individuative-Reflective* – (usually mid-twenties to late thirties): This is the tough stage, often begun in young adulthood, when people start seeing outside the box and realizing that there are other "boxes." They begin to examine their beliefs critically on their own and often become disillusioned with their former faith. Ironically, the Stage 3 people usually think that Stage 4 people have become "backsliders" when in reality they have actually moved forward.

Stage 5: *Conjunctive Faith* – (mid-life crisis): It is rare for people to reach this stage before mid-life. This is the point when people begin to realize the limits of logic and start to accept life's paradoxes. As they begin to see life as a mystery, they often return to sacred stories and symbols but this time without remaining in a theological box.

Stage 6: *Universalizing Faith* – (enlightened stage): Few people reach this stage; those who do, live their lives to the full in service of others without real worry or spiritual doubt.

Simplified Version by M. Scott Peck (A Different Drum, 1987)

Chaotic-Antisocial – People in this stage are usually self-centered and often find themselves in trouble due to unprincipled living. If they do finally embrace the next stage, it often occurs in a very dramatic way.

Formal-Institutional – At this stage people rely on some sort of institution (such as a church) to give them stability. They become attached to the forms of their religion and become extremely upset when these are called into question.

Skeptic-Individual – Those who break with the previous stage usually do so when they start seriously questioning previously held values and beliefs. Frequently they end up non-religious and some stay here permanently.

Mystical-Communal – People who reach this stage start to realize that there is truth to be found in both the previous two stages and that life can be paradoxical and mysterious. Emphasis is placed more on community rather than on individual concerns.

Bibliography

Anderson, Bernhard W. *Contours of Old Testament Theology*. Minneapolis: Fortress, 1999.
———. *Creation versus Chaos*. New York: Association Press, 1967.
———. *Rediscovering the Bible*. New York: Association Press, 1951.
Armstrong, Karen. *The Case for God*. New York: Anchor, 2010.
———. *A Short History of Myth*. New York: Canongate, 2005.
Borg, Marcus J. *The God We Never Knew*. New York: HarperSanFrancisco, 1998.
———. *The Heart of Christianity*. New York: HarperSanFrancisco, 2004.
———. *Meeting Jesus Again for the First Time*. New York: HarperSanFrancisco, 1994.
———. *Reading the Bible Again for the First Time*. New York: HarperSanFrancisco, 2001.
———. *Speaking Christian*. New York: HarperOne, 2011.
Borg, Marcus J., and N. T. Wright. *The Meaning of Jesus: Two Visions*. New York: HarperSanFrancisco, 1999.
Boring, M. Eugene. *Revelation*. Interpretation: A Bible Commentary for Teaching and Preaching. Louisville: John Knox, 1989.
Bowne, Dale R., and John D. Currid. "Biblical Society: A Covenantal Society." In *Building a Christian World View*, edited by W. Andrew Hoffecker, 2:156–85. Phillipsburg, NJ: Presbyterian and Reformed, 1988.
Brueggemann, Walter. *Genesis*. Interpretation: A Bible Commentary for Teaching and Preaching. Atlanta: John Knox, 1982.
Bultmann, Rudolf. *The Gospel of John: A Commentary*. Translated by G. R. Beasley-Murray, R. W. N. Hoare, and J. K. Riches. Philadelphia: Westminster, 1971.
Cahill, Thomas. *Desire of the Everlasting Hills*. New York: Anchor, 2001.
Caird, G. B., and L. D. Hurst. *New Testament Theology*. Oxford: Clarendon, 1994.
Clayton, Philip, and Arthur Peacocke. *In Whom We Live and Move and Have our Being: Panentheistic Reflections on God's Presence in a Scientific World* Grand Rapids, MI: Eerdmans, 2004.
Countryman, L. William, *Biblical Authority or Biblical Tyranny? Scripture and the Christian Pilgrimage*. Valley Forge: PA: Trinity International, 1994.
Creed, John M. *The Divinity of Jesus Christ*. Fontana ed. London: Collins, 1964 [1938].
Dobzhansky, Theodosius. "Nothing in Biology Makes Sense Except in the Light of Evolution," *The American Biology Teacher* 35 (1973) 125–29. Online: http://people delphiforums.com/lordorman/light.htm.
Drane, John. *Introducing the New Testament*. Revised and Updated. Minneapolis: Fortress, 2001.

BIBLIOGRAPHY

Edwards, Denis. *The God of Evolution: A Trinitarian Theology*. Mahway, NJ: Paulist, 1999.
Ehrman, Bart. *How Jesus Became God*. New York: HarperOne, 2014.
Fox, Matthew. *Creation Spirituality*. New York: HarperSanFrancisco, 1991.
———. *Original Blessing*. Santa Fe, NM: Bear & Co., 1983.
Griffin, David Ray. *Reenchantment without Supernaturalism: A Process Philosophy of Religion*. Ithaca, NY: Cornell University Press, 2001.
Hamilton, William. *The New Essence of Christianity*. New York: Association, 1966.
Haught, John F. *Deeper Than Darwin: The Prospect for Religion in the Age of Evolution*. Boulder, CO: Westview, 2003.
———. *God After Darwin: A Theology of Evolution*. Boulder, CO: Westview, 2000.
———. *The Promise of Nature: Ecology and Cosmic Purpose*. Mahwah, NJ: Paulist, 1993.
———. *Responses to 101 Questions on God and Evolution*. Mahwah, NJ: Paulist, 2001.
———. *Science and Religion: From Conflict to Conversation*. Mahwah, NJ: Paulist, 1995.
———. *What is God? How to Think About the Divine*. Mahwah, NJ: Paulist, 1986.
Jones, Van. "8 Questions," *TIME* 191 (January 29, 2018) 56.
Knox, John. *The Humanity and Divinity of Christ*. Cambridge: Cambridge University Press. 1967.
Küng, Hans. *Does God Exist?* Translated by Edward Quinn. New York: Doubleday, 1980.
Livingstone, David N. *Darwin's Forgotten Defenders: The Encounter between Evangelical Theology and Evolutionary Thought*. Grand Rapids, MI: Eerdmans, 1967.
Mackintosh, H. R. *The Doctrine of the Person of Jesus Christ*. Edinburgh: T. & T. Clark, 1913.
McGrath, Alister E. *Christian Theology: An Introduction*. 5th. ed. Malden, MA: Wiley-Blackwell, 2011.
McLaren, Brian D. *A Generous Orthodoxy*. Grand Rapids, MI: Zondervan, 2004.
———. *A New Kind of Christian: A Tale of Two Friends on a Spiritual Journey*. San Francisco: Jossey-Bass, 2001.
———. *A New Kind of Christianity: Ten Questions That Are Transforming the Faith*. New York: HarperCollins, 2010.
Moltmann, Jürgen. *God in Creation: A New Theology of Creation and the Spirit of God*. Minneapolis, MN: Fortress, 1993.
Noll, Mark A., and David Livingstone. "Charles Hodge and B. B. Warfield on Science, the Bible, Evolution, and Darwinism." In *Perspectives on an Evolving Creation*, edited by Keith B. Miller, 61–71. Grand Rapids, MI: Eerdmans, 2003.
Peacocke, Arthur. "Biological Evolution—A Positive Theological Appraisal." In *Evolutionary and Molecular Biology: Scientific Perspectives on Divine Action*. Edited by R. J. Russell et al., 357–76. Vatican City: Vatican Observatory, 1998.
———. *Theology for a Scientific Age: Being and Becoming—Natural, Divine, and Human*. Minneapolis, MN: Fortress, 1993.
Rice, Alan W. "The Cosmology of Modern Science." In *Building a Christian World View*, edited by W. Andrew Hoffecker, 2:71–111. Phillipsburg, NJ: Presbyterian and Reformed, 1988.
Richardson, Alan. *Genesis I–XI*. Torch Commentary. London: SCM, 1953.
Ruse, Michael. *Can a Darwinian Be a Christian?* Cambridge: Cambridge University Press, 2001.
Sanders, E. P. *Jesus and Judaism*. Philadelphia: Fortress, 1985.
———. "Jesus: His Religious Type," *Reflections* 87 (1992) 4–12.

BIBLIOGRAPHY

Schneider, Robert J. "Science and Faith: Perspectives on Christianity and Science." No pages. Online: http://community.berea.edu/scienceandfaith/default.asp.

Schulweis, Harold M. *For Those Who Can't Believe*. New York: HarperPerennial, 1995.

Schweitzer, Albert. *The Quest of the Historical Jesus*. New York: Macmillan, 1968.

Smith, Huston. *Forgotten Truth: The Common Vision of the World's Religions*. New York: HarperSanFrancisco, 1976.

Spong, John Shelby. *Eternal Life: A New Vision*. New York: HarperOne, 2009.

———. *Liberating the Gospels: Reading the Bible with Jewish Eyes*. San Francisco: HarperSanFrancisco, 1996.

———. *A New Kind of Christianity for a New World*. New York: HarperOne, 2001.

———. *Rescuing the Bible from Fundamentalism*. New York: HarperSanFrancisco, 1991.

———. *The Sins of Scripture*. New York: HarperOne, 2006.

———. *Why Christianity Must Change or Die*. New York: HarperOne, 1999.

Vande Kappelle, Robert P. *Beyond Belief: Faith, Science, and the Value of Unknowing*. Eugene: OR: Wipf & Stock, 2012.

———. *Iron Sharpens Iron*. Eugene: OR: Wipf & Stock, 2013.

———. *The Scandal of Divine Love*. Eugene, OR: Wipf & Stock, 2017.

———. *Securing Life: The Enduring Message of the Bible*. Eugene, OR: Wipf & Stock, 2015.

Walls, Andrew F. *The Cross-Cultural Process in Christian History*. Maryknoll, NY: Orbis, 2002.

———. *The Missionary Movement in Christian History: Studies in the Transmission of Faith*. Maryknoll, NY: Orbis, 1996.

Whitehead, Alfred North. *Process and Reality*. Revised edition. New York: Free Press, 1978.

———. *Religion in the Making*. New York: Fordham University Press, 1996.

———. *Science and the Modern World*. New York: Free Press, 1967.

Williams, Patricia A. *Doing without Adam and Eve: Sociobiology and Original Sin*. Minneapolis: Fortress, 2001.

Witherington III, Ben. *Jesus the Sage: The Pilgrimage of Wisdom*. Minneapolis: Fortress, 1994.

———. *John's Wisdom: A Commentary on the Fourth Gospel*. Louisville: Westminster John Knox, 1995.

Wright, Robert. *The Evolution of God*. New York: Little, Brown, 2009.

Subject/Name Index

Abraham (patriarch), 89, 151, 153, 154–55
Adam and Eve, 57, 89, 110, 115, 116–19, 126, 132
afterlife, doctrine of the, 134–37, 147
animism, 33
Anselm of Canterbury, 131
apocalypticism, 123, 136–37, 137–39, 147
   and Synoptic Apocalypse, 138
apophatic, 22, 40n14
Aquinas, Thomas, 31
Armstrong, Karen, 2cn2, 29, 86
atheism, 33
atonement, doctrine of the, 131
Augustine (bishop), 22
   and evolution, 93–95, 102
   and original sin, 116, 117, 118–19
   and principle of accommodation, 94
   and privation, 114–16

Barth, Karl, 31
Bonhoeffer, Dietrich, 10, 39, 59–60
Borg, Marcus, 17, 22n4, 29, 36, 51–52, 54–55, 79n7, 131, 131n1, 147n8
Bultmann, Rudolph, 142

Cahill, Thomas, 158
Calvin, John, 60, 69, 97
canonical process, 72–75

Chalcedon, Council of, 59
Christology, 60–61
   adoptionist, 49–50
   from above, 47
   from below, 46, 47
   See also Jesus Christ
church, doctrine of the, 150–63
   four notes of the, 159–60
corporate personality, 151
cosmogony, 92n7
Countryman, William, 67
creation, doctrine of, 38, 82–107, 143
   and design. *See* design, cosmic
   and Genesis, 83–90
   and stewardship, 89–90
   and worship, 86–89
creationism, 92–93, 93n9, 119
Creed, J. M., 60

Dana, James, 97
Dante Alighieri, 136
Daoism, 21
Darwin, Charles, 30, 96–97, 98, 100, 101, 118
Denys the Areopagite, 22
design, cosmic, 100–105
dialectical method, 10, 13, 15, 19
discipleship, 78, 127, 146, 153
Dobzhansky, Theodosius, 95–96

Subject/Name Index

Easter, 51–52
Eckhart, Meister, 91, 143
Edwards, Denis, 98
Ehrman, Bart, 59
election, doctrine of, 152, 154–55
Enuma Elish, 89
Erikson, Erik, 4
eschatology, 144–45
   Christian, 54, 55–56, 138–41
   inaugurated, 138, 141
   Jewish, 52–53, 137–38
   realized, 138, 141–42, 145–46
eternal life, 142–43
Evagrius of Pontus, 22
evil, doctrine of, 108–28
   and free will, 115–16
   as privation, 115–16
   moral, 109–10
   natural, 111–12
   reality of, 112–14
   source of, 114–20
   See also sin, original
evolution
   biological, 30, 95–98, 100, 101, 102–4, 117–20
   theistic, 93–98

faith, 17–28
   meaning of, 22–27
   stages of, 4–5, 165–66
Fall, doctrine of the, 132
fall-redemption model, 147, 148
Fowler, James, 4, 165–66
Fox, Matthew, 148
free will, 114
fundamentalism, 2, 70

Gardner, Howard, 20
gnostic, 73–74
God, 13, 29–42
   and supernatural theism, 13, 30, 31–32
   as personal, 31
   knowledge of, 31
   monarchical model of, 36, 37, 82, 91, 108–9, 129–30, 150–51
   Spirit model of, 36–40, 82, 91, 108–9, 129–30, 150–51

   views of, 30–40
Gospels, reliability of, 51–52
Gray, Asa, 97
Griffin, David Ray, 33

Haught, John, 99, 102–3
heaven, doctrine of, 143–44
Hegel, Georg W. F., 10, 15
hell, reality of, 120–23
Hengel, Martin, 59
henotheism, 33
Herder, Johann G. von, 69
Hick, John, 29
higher criticism, 70
history, end of, 144–47

imago dei (image of God), 57
incarnation, 5–6, 116
Islam, 3, 7

James, William, 50
Jesus Christ, 43–62
   and eschatology, 53–56
   as human bridge to God, 56–60
   as Lord, 46–52
   Christ of faith, 44, 51–52
   divinity of, 46–47
   historical Jesus, 48, 49–51
   humanity of, 46–47, 48–52
   Jewish images of, 52–56
   second coming of, 144–48
   titles of, 48, 51, 52, 58
   triple office of, 60–61
John the Baptist, 50, 53, 140
Jones, Van, 2
Jung, Carl, 58

kataphatic, 40n15
Kepler, Johannes, 19–20
Kierkegaard, Søren, 7, 11, 12, 15, 152–53
kingdom of God, 53, 138, 139–41, 142, 143
   paradoxical nature of, 139–40
knowing, ways of, 20–22
   logos, 20–22
   mythos, 20–22
Knox, John, 49

Subject/Name Index

Kohlberg, Lawrence, 4
Küng, Hans, 103

Lessing, G. E., 15
Lewis, C. S., 46
liberalism, 60, 70
Loftus, James, 13
love, 146
Luther, Martin, 47, 68–69

Maccabean period, 123, 135
Manichaeism, 115
Marcion, 74
marriage, biblical institution of, 90
Maximus the Confessor, 22
McCosh, James, 97
McGrath, Alistair, 133–34
McLaren, Brian, 30
Mill, John Stuart, 22
Milton, John, 126
Moltmann, Jürgen, 34
monovision, 14–15
myth, 20–21
   in Genesis, 86

Napoleon Bonaparte, 43–44
Newman, John Henry, 60
New Testament, 44–46
Nicene Creed, 59

open universe, 92–98
Origen of Alexandria, 22
original goodness, 148
original sin. *See* sin, original
Orr, James, 96–97
Outsider Test for Faith, 11

pain and suffering, 110–11
panentheism, 33, 34
pantheism, 33, 113
Paul (apostle), 10, 26, 44, 60, 72, 73,
   112, 136, 141, 145
  and original sin, 116–17
  and women, 158–59
Peacocke, Arthur, 34
Peck, M. Scott, 166
Phillips, J. B., 40
Piaget, Jean, 4

pietism, 70
polytheism, 33
Postcritical Paradigm, 18–19, 78–80
postmodernism, 22
prayer, 160–61
Precritical Paradigm, 18–19, 46, 147
promise, cosmic, 100–105

"rapture" of believers, 145, 146
reality
  levels of, 4, 105–6
reason, 3
religion and science
  biological evolution and, 90–98
  cosmic promise, 100–105
  models of, 98–100
Renan, Ernst, 43
resurrection, doctrine of, 135
Richardson, Alan, 88

Sabbath, 93, 157
salvation, doctrine of, 119, 120, 132–34,
   147
  definition of, 132–33
  the cross and, 130–32
Sanders, E. P., 53–54
Satan (the devil; Lucifer), 115, 123–24
  and the book of Revelation, 124–26
  and the Gospel of John, 126–27
Schulweis, Harold, 32
Schumacher, E. F., 91
Schweitzer, Albert, 45
science and religion. *See* religion and
   science
scripture, 3, 63–81
  as story, 75–78
  inspiration of, 64, 65–67
  interpretation of, 68–72
Second Coming. *See* Jesus Christ, second coming of
selfhood
  levels of, 4, 105–6
Sermon on the Mount, 161
sin, doctrine of, 38, 108–28
  original, 110, 116–20, 132, 147
Smith, Huston, 4
  levels of reality and selfhood, 105–6

Subject/Name Index

Spong, John Shelby, 30, 32, 40, 161
story theology, 75–78
suffering. *See* pain and suffering

Teilhard de Chardin, Pierre, 96
Ten Commandments, 64
theistic evolution. *See* evolution, theistic
theodicy, 112
theology
   objective, 11, 12
   sources of, 3
   subjective, 11, 12
Tillich, Paul, 39
tradition, 3
translation principle, 5–7

truth, 9–16

ultimate questions, 1

Walls, Andrew, 5–7
Warfield, Benjamin B., 97
Wells, H. G., 44
Wesleyan Quadrilateral, 3
Whitehead, Alfred North, 33, 35, 39, 91, 98
Williams, Patricia, 117, 118
Wright, Robert, 148

Zen Buddhism, 22
Zoroaster, 122

www.ingramcontent.com/pod-product-compliance
Lightning Source LLC
Chambersburg PA
CBHW070922180426
43192CB00037B/1677